fabulous
first courses

70 fabulous first courses

Soups, appetizers, salads and other delicious ways to start the meal

Christine Ingram

southwater

This edition is published by Southwater

Southwater is an imprint of Anness Publishing Ltd
Hermes House, 88–89 Blackfriars Road, London SE1 8HA
tel. 020 7401 2077; fax 020 7633 9499
www.southwaterbooks.com; info@anness.com

© Anness Publishing Ltd 2005

UK agent: The Manning Partnership Ltd
6 The Old Dairy, Melcombe Road, Bath BA2 3LR
tel. 01225 478444; fax 01225 478440
sales@manning-partnership.co.uk

UK distributor: Grantham Book Services Ltd
Isaac Newton Way, Alma Park Industrial Estate
Grantham, Lincs NG31 9SD
tel. 01476 541080; fax 01476 541061; orders@gbs.tbs-ltd.co.uk

North American agent/distributor: National Book Network
4501 Forbes Boulevard, Suite 200, Lanham, MD 20706
tel. 301 459 3366; fax 301 429 5746; www.nbnbooks.com

Australian agent/distributor: Pan Macmillan Australia
Level 18, St Martins Tower, 31 Market St, Sydney, NSW 2000
tel. 1300 135 113; fax 1300 135 103
customer.service@macmillan.com.au

New Zealand agent/distributor: David Bateman Ltd
30 Tarndale Grove, Off Bush Road, Albany, Auckland
tel. (09) 415 7664; fax (09) 415 8892

All rights reserved. No part of this publication may be reproduced, stored in a retrieval system, or transmitted in any way or by any means, electronic, mechanical, photocopying, recording or otherwise, without the prior written permission of the copyright holder.

A CIP catalogue record for this book is available from the British Library.

Publisher: Joanna Lorenz
Editorial Director: Helen Sudell
Editors: Charlotte Berman and Elizabeth Woodland
Designer: Bill Mason, Jane Coney
Cover Designer: Whitelight Design Associates
Production Controller: Claire Rae

Previously published as part of a larger volume, *First Impressions*

1 3 5 7 9 10 8 6 4 2

NOTES

Bracketed terms are for American readers.

For all recipes, quantities are given in both metric and imperial measures and, where appropriate, measures are also given in standard cups and spoons. Follow one set, but not a mixture because they are not interchangeable.

Standard spoon and cup measures are level.
1 tsp = 5ml, 1 tbsp = 15ml
1 cup = 250ml/8fl oz

Australian standard tablespoons are 20ml. Australian readers should use 3 tsp in place of 1 tbsp for measuring small quantities of gelatine, cornflour, salt etc.

Medium (US large) eggs are used unless otherwise stated.

Contents

Introduction 6

Soups 8

Pâtés, Terrines & Soufflés 26

Pastries, Tartlets & Toasts 44

Fish, Meat & Poultry Appetizers 60

Vegetarian Dishes 80

Index 96

Introduction

First courses are the perfect prelude to any main meal. They need to be satisfying without being too filling: a successful appetizer leaves the guests hungry for more, and it also sets the dinner mood, stimulates the appetite, and promises that exciting things are to come. The dish can be as simple or elaborate and as rich or refreshing as you desire – the only rule is to make sure that your first course creates a fantastic impression.

The variety of appetizers is almost endless. If it's a sophisticated dish suitable for an elegant dinner party that you require, then you can choose from a refreshing soup, such as Chilled Prawn and Cucumber Soup, a delicate Sea Trout Mousse, or something more unusual, such as Smoked Salmon and Rice Salad Parcels. Alternatively, for a more informal occasion you might want to make a classic Caesar Salad, a succulent Risotto with Four Cheeses or a tasty Herbed Liver Pâté Pie. Delicious vegetarian choices include Leek and Onion Tartlets and Greek Aubergine and Spinach Pie, which can both be served either warm or cold, so you can prepare them in advance if you like.

Your choice of first course should take its cue from the food you intend to serve as a main course. Choose with care, as the appetizer will set the tone for the rest of the meal. If you are serving a roast meat or heavy stew as the main course, select something fairly light, such as Hot Crab Soufflés, or Marinated Asparagus and Langoustines. If, on the other hand, you are grilling fish or chicken you could decide on something richer and more filling, such as Creamy Courgette and Dolcelatte Soup or Egg and Salmon Puff Parcels.

Don't be afraid to mix and match appetizers with main courses from different cuisines – for example, Malaysian Prawn Laksa would go well with a French or Italian-style main course, and Cannellini Bean and Rosemary Bruschetta or Crab and Ricotta Tartlets could happily come before a creamy curry or a Mexican dish – it's taste and texture that are the important factors to take into consideration.

There are over seventy delicious appetizers in this book, so whether you want soups or salads, meat or fish, hot or cold dishes or classic or exotic recipes, there's a first course here to match any main course and to impress every guest.

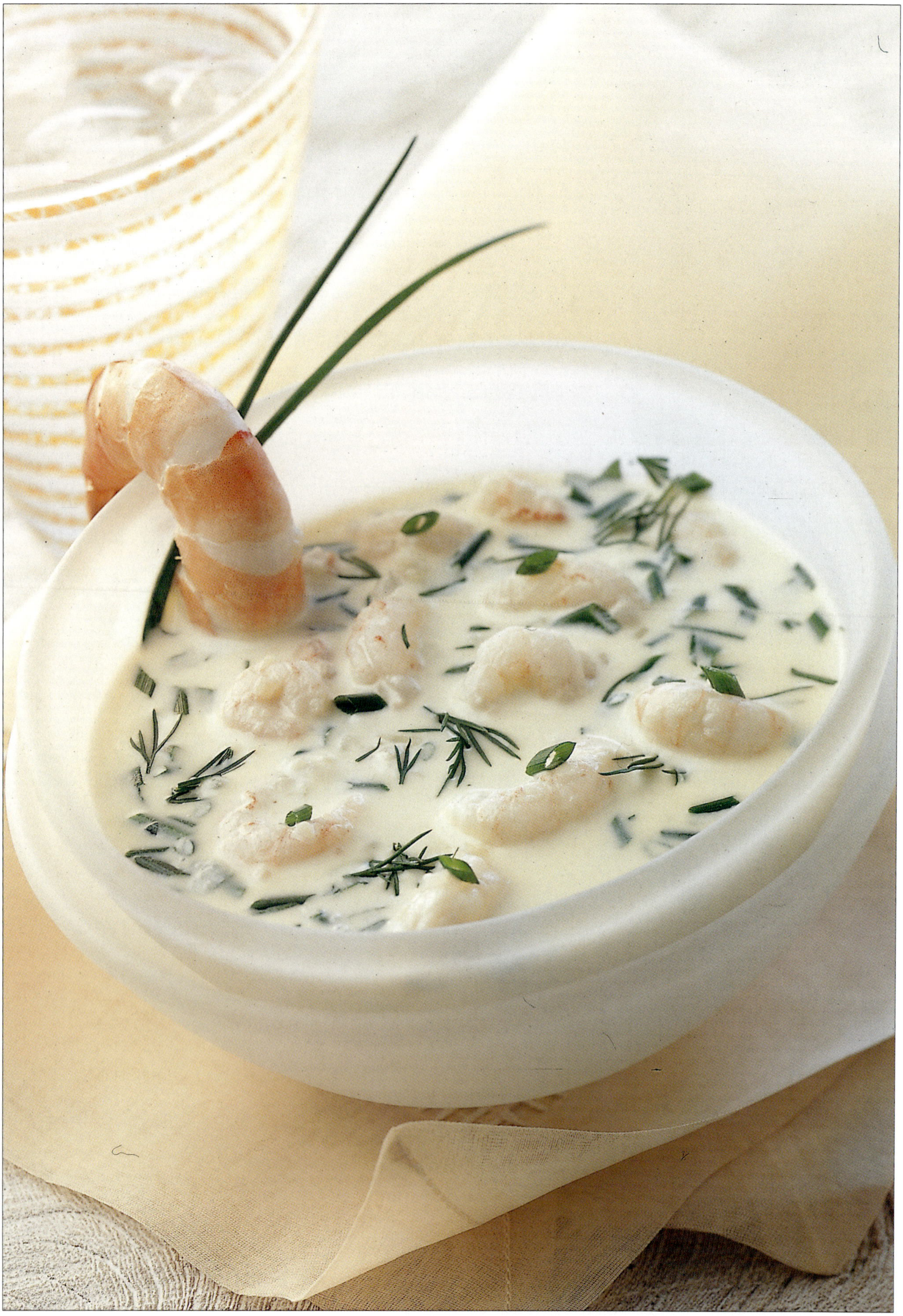

Soups

Whether a refreshing, chilled dish, such as Cold Cucumber and Yogurt Soup, or a delicious French classic such as Fish Soup with Rouille, or a spicy Malaysian Prawn Laksa, soups are always a popular way of starting a gourmet meal.

Cold Cucumber and Yogurt Soup

This refreshing cold soup uses the classic combination of cucumber and yogurt, with the added flavours of garlic and crunchy walnuts.

Serves 5–6

1 cucumber
4 garlic cloves
2.5ml/½ tsp salt
75g/3oz/¾ cup walnut pieces
40g/1½oz day-old bread, torn into pieces
30ml/2 tbsp walnut or sunflower oil
400ml/14fl oz/1⅔ cups sheep's or
   cow's yogurt
120ml/4fl oz/½ cup cold water or
   chilled still mineral water
5–10ml/1–2 tsp lemon juice
40g/1½oz/scant ½ cup walnuts,
   chopped, to garnish
olive oil, for drizzling
fresh dill sprigs, to garnish

1 Cut the cucumber into two and peel one half of it. Dice the cucumber flesh and set aside.

2 Using a large pestle and mortar, crush the garlic and salt together well, then add the walnuts and bread.

3 When the mixture is smooth, add the walnut or sunflower oil slowly and combine well.

4 Transfer the walnut and bread mixture to a large bowl, then beat in the cow's or sheep's yogurt and the diced cucumber.

5 Add the cold water or mineral water and lemon juice to taste. Chill until ready to serve.

6 Ladle the soup into chilled soup bowls to serve. Garnish with the chopped walnuts, drizzling a little olive oil over them, and with sprigs of dill.

COOK'S TIP
If you prefer your soup smooth, purée it in a food processor or blender before serving.

Chilled Tomato and Sweet Pepper Soup

This recipe was inspired by the Spanish gazpacho, the difference being that this soup is cooked first, and then chilled.

Serves 4

2 red (bell) peppers, halved and seeded
45ml/3 tbsp olive oil
1 onion, finely chopped
2 garlic cloves, crushed
675g/1½lb ripe well-flavoured tomatoes
150ml/¼ pint/⅔ cup red wine
600ml/1 pint/2½ cups chicken stock
salt and ground black pepper
chopped fresh chives, to garnish

For the croûtons
2 slices white bread, crusts removed
60ml/4 tbsp olive oil

1 Cut each red pepper half into quarters. Place skin side up on a grill (broiler) rack and cook until the skins are charred. Transfer to a bowl and cover with a plate or put into a plastic bag and seal.

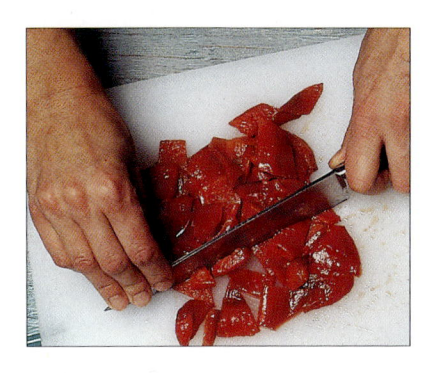

2 Heat the oil in a large pan. Add the onion and garlic and cook over a low heat, stirring occasionally, for about 5 minutes, until soft. Meanwhile, remove the skin from the peppers and coarsely chop the flesh. Cut the tomatoes into chunks.

3 Add the peppers and tomatoes to the pan, then cover and cook gently for 10 minutes. Add the wine and cook for a further 5 minutes, then add the stock and season with salt and pepper to taste and continue to simmer for 20 minutes.

4 To make the croûtons, cut the bread into cubes. Heat the oil in a small frying pan, add the bread and cook, stirring and tossing frequently, until golden brown all over. Drain well on kitchen paper, leave to cool and then store in an airtight box until you are ready to serve.

5 Process the soup in a blender or food processor until smooth. Pour it into a clean glass or ceramic bowl, cover with clear film (plastic wrap) and leave to cool thoroughly before chilling in the refrigerator for at least 3 hours. When the soup is cold, taste and adjust the seasoning, if necessary.

6 Serve the soup in bowls, topped with the croûtons and garnished with chopped chives.

Pear and Watercress Soup

The pears in the soup are complemented beautifully by Stilton croûtons.

Serves 6

1 bunch watercress
4 pears, sliced
900ml/1½ pints/3¾ cups chicken stock
120ml/4fl oz/½ cup double (heavy) cream
juice of 1 lime
salt and ground black pepper

For the croûtons
25g/1oz/2 tbsp butter
15ml/1 tbsp olive oil
200g/7oz/3 cups cubed stale bread
150g/5oz/1 cup chopped Stilton

1 Reserve about one-third of the watercress leaves. Place the rest of the leaves and stalks in a pan with the pear slices, stock and a little salt and pepper. Simmer gently for about 15–20 minutes. Set aside some of the reserved watercress leaves for garnishing, then add the rest of the leaves to the soup. Process in a blender or food processor until smooth.

2 Put the mixture into a bowl and stir in the cream and the lime juice to mix the flavours thoroughly. Season again to taste. Pour all the soup back into a pan and reheat, stirring gently until warmed through.

3 To make the croûtons, melt the butter and oil in a frying pan. Add the bread cubes and cook, stirring and tossing them frequently, until golden brown. Drain well on kitchen paper.

4 Spread them out on a baking sheet, sprinkle the cheese over them and heat under a hot grill (broiler) until bubbling. Reheat the soup and pour into bowls. Divide the croûtons and the reserved watercress leaves among them and serve immediately.

Broccoli Soup with Garlic Toast

This is an Italian recipe, originating from Rome. For the best flavour and brightest colour, use the freshest broccoli you can find.

Serves 6

675g/1½ lb broccoli spears
1.75 litres/3 pints/7½ cups chicken or vegetable stock
30ml/2 tbsp fresh lemon juice
salt and ground black pepper
freshly grated Parmesan cheese (optional), to serve

For the garlic toast
6 slices white bread
1 large garlic clove, halved

1 Using a small sharp knife, peel the broccoli stems, starting from the base of the stalks and pulling gently up towards the florets. (The peel comes off very easily.) Chop the broccoli into small chunks.

2 Bring the stock to the boil in a large pan over a medium heat. Add the chopped broccoli, lower the heat and simmer for 30 minutes, or until soft.

COOK'S TIP
As this is an Italian recipe, choose a really good-quality Parmesan cheese, if you are using it. The very best is Italy's own Parmigiano-Reggiano. Alternatively, as it is Roman, substitute Pecorino Romano, which is made from sheep's milk. Both should be freshly grated.

3 Remove the pan from the heat and leave the soup to cool slightly, then transfer about half of it to a blender or food processor. Process to a smooth purée. Return the puréed soup to the pan and mix it into the rest of the soup. Stir in lemon juice and season to taste with salt and pepper.

4 Just before serving, gently reheat the soup to just below boiling point. Toast the bread, rub with the cut surfaces of the garlic and cut into quarters. Place three or four pieces of toast in the base of each soup plate. Ladle on the soup. Serve immediately, with grated Parmesan cheese if you like.

Spanish Garlic Soup

This is a simple and satisfying soup, made with one of the most popular ingredients in the Mediterranean region – garlic.

Serves 4

30ml/2 tbsp olive oil
4 large garlic cloves, peeled
4 slices French bread, 5mm/¼ in thick
15ml/1 tbsp paprika
1 litre/1¾ pints/4 cups beef stock
1.5ml/¼ tsp ground cumin
pinch of saffron threads
4 eggs
salt and ground black pepper
chopped fresh parsley, to garnish

1 Preheat the oven to 230°C/450°F/Gas 8. Heat the oil in a large pan. Add the whole garlic cloves and cook over a low heat until golden. Remove with a slotted spoon and set aside.

2 Add the bread to the pan and cook on both sides until golden. Remove from the pan and set aside.

3 Add the paprika to the pan and cook for a few seconds, stirring constantly. Stir in the beef stock, cumin and saffron, then add the reserved fried garlic, crushing the cloves with the back of a wooden spoon. Season with salt and ground black pepper to taste then cook over a low heat for about 5 minutes.

4 Ladle the soup into four individual ovenproof bowls and gently break an egg into each one. Place the slices of fried French bread on top of the eggs and place the bowls in the oven for about 3–4 minutes, or until the eggs are just set. Sprinkle with chopped fresh parsley to garnish and serve the soup immediately.

COOK'S TIP
Use home-made beef stock for the best flavour or buy prepared chilled stock from your supermarket. Never use stock (bouillon) cubes as most of them contain too much salt.

Tortellini Chanterelle Broth

The savoury-sweet quality of chanterelle mushrooms combines well in a simple broth with spinach-and-ricotta-filled tortellini. The addition of a little sherry creates a lovely warming effect.

Serves 4

1.2 litres/2 pints/5 cups chicken stock
75ml/5 tbsp dry sherry
175g/6oz fresh chanterelle mushrooms, trimmed and sliced, or 15g/½ oz/½ cup dried chanterelles
350g/12oz fresh spinach and ricotta tortellini, or 175g/6oz dried
chopped fresh parsley, to garnish

1 Bring the chicken stock to the boil, add the dry sherry and fresh or dried mushrooms and simmer over a low heat for 10 minutes.

2 Cook the tortellini according to the packet instructions.

3 Drain the tortellini, add to the stock and mushroom mixture, then ladle the broth into four warmed soup bowls, making sure each contains the about same proportions of tortellini and mushrooms. Garnish with the chopped parsley and serve immediately.

French Onion and Morel Soup

French onion soup is appreciated for its light beefy taste. There are few improvements to be made to this classic soup, but a few richly scented morel mushrooms will impart a worthwhile flavour.

Serves 4

50g/2oz/4 tbsp unsalted (sweet) butter, plus extra for spreading
15ml/1 tbsp vegetable oil
3 onions, sliced
900ml/1½ pints/3¾ cups beef stock
75ml/5 tbsp Madeira or sherry
8 dried morel mushrooms
4 slices French bread
75g/3oz Gruyère, Beaufort or Fontina cheese, grated
30ml/2 tbsp chopped fresh parsley

1 Melt the butter with the oil in a large frying pan, then add the sliced onions and cook over a low heat for 10–15 minutes, until the onions are a rich mahogany brown colour.

2 Transfer the browned onions to a large pan, pour in the beef stock, add the Madeira or sherry and the dried morels, then simmer for 20 minutes.

3 Preheat the grill (broiler) to medium and toast the French bread on both sides. Spread one side with butter and heap with the grated cheese.

4 Ladle the soup into four flameproof bowls, float the cheese-topped toasts on top and grill (broil) until they are crisp and brown and the cheese is bubbling. Alternatively, grill the cheese-topped toast, then place one slice in each warmed soup bowl before ladling the hot soup over it. The toast will float to the surface. Sprinkle over the chopped fresh parsley and serve.

COOK'S TIP
The flavour and richness of this soup will improve with keeping. Store in the refrigerator for up to 5 days.

Fresh Tomato Soup

Intensely flavoured sun-ripened tomatoes need little embellishment in this fresh-tasting soup. If you buy from the supermarket, choose the juiciest looking ones and add the amount of sugar and vinegar necessary, depending on their natural sweetness.

Serves 6

1.3–1.6kg/3–3½ lb ripe tomatoes
400ml/14fl oz/1⅔ cups chicken or vegetable stock
45ml/3 tbsp sun-dried tomato paste
30–45ml/2–3 tbsp balsamic vinegar
10–15ml/2–3 tsp caster (superfine) sugar
small handful of basil leaves
salt and ground black pepper
basil leaves, to garnish
toasted cheese croûtes and crème fraîche, to serve

1 Plunge the tomatoes into boiling water for 30 seconds, then refresh in cold water. Peel off the skins and quarter the tomatoes. Put them in a large, heavy pan and pour over the chicken or vegetable stock. Bring just to the boil, reduce the heat, cover and simmer the mixture gently for about 10 minutes, until the tomatoes are thickened and pulpy.

2 Stir in the tomato paste, vinegar, sugar and basil. Season with salt and pepper, then cook gently, stirring, for 2 minutes. Process the soup in a blender or food processor, then return to the pan and reheat gently.

3 Serve in bowls topped with one or two toasted cheese croûtes and a spoonful of crème fraîche, garnished with basil leaves.

COOK'S TIP
This Italian soup may be left to cool and then chilled in the refrigerator before serving on a hot day.

Hungarian Sour Cherry Soup

Particularly popular in summer, this fruit soup is typical of Hungarian cooking. The recipe makes good use of plump, sour cherries. Fruit soups are thickened with flour, and a touch of salt is added to help bring out the flavour of the cold soup.

Serves 4

15ml/1 tbsp plain (all-purpose) flour
120ml/4fl oz/½ cup sour cream
a generous pinch of salt
5ml/1 tsp caster (superfine) sugar
225g/8oz/1½ cups fresh sour or morello cherries, pitted
900ml/1½ pints/3¾ cups water
50g/2oz/¼ cup granulated sugar

1 In a bowl, blend the flour with the sour cream until completely smooth, then add the salt and caster sugar.

2 Put the cherries in a pan with the water and granulated sugar. Gently poach for about 10 minutes.

3 Remove from the heat and set aside 30ml/2 tbsp of the cooking liquid as a garnish. Stir another 30ml/2 tbsp of the cherry liquid into the flour and sour cream mixture, then pour this on to the cherries.

4 Return to the heat. Bring to the boil, then simmer gently for 5–6 minutes.

5 Remove from the heat, cover with clear film (plastic wrap) and leave to cool. Add extra salt if necessary. Serve with the reserved cooking liquid swirled in.

Creamy Courgette and Dolcelatte Soup

The beauty of this soup is its delicate colour, its creamy texture and its subtle taste. But if you prefer a more pronounced cheese flavour, use Gorgonzola instead of Dolcelatte.

Serves 4–6

30ml/2 tbsp olive oil
15g/½oz/1 tbsp butter
1 onion, coarsely chopped
900g/2lb courgettes (zucchini), sliced
5ml/1 tsp dried oregano
about 600ml/1 pint/2½ cups vegetable stock
115g/4 oz Dolcelatte cheese, diced
300ml/½ pint/1¼ cups single (light) cream
salt and ground black pepper

To garnish
fresh oregano sprigs
extra Dolcelatte cheese

1 Heat the olive oil and butter in a large, heavy pan until foaming. Add the onion and cook over a medium heat for about 5 minutes, stirring frequently, until softened, but not brown.

2 Add the courgettes and oregano and season with salt and pepper to taste. Cook over a medium heat for 10 minutes, stirring frequently.

3 Pour in the stock and bring to the boil, stirring frequently. Lower the heat, half-cover the pan and simmer gently, stirring occasionally, for about 30 minutes. Stir in the diced Dolcelatte until it is melted.

4 Process the soup in a blender or food processor until smooth, then press through a sieve into a clean pan.

5 Add two-thirds of the cream and stir over a low heat until hot, but not boiling. Check the consistency and add more stock if the soup is too thick. Taste and adjust the seasoning if necessary.

6 Pour into heated bowls. Swirl in the remaining cream, garnish with fresh oregano and extra Dolcelatte cheese, crumbled, and serve immediately.

Spinach and Tofu Soup

This soup is really delicious. If fresh spinach is not in season, watercress or lettuce can be used instead.

Serves 4

1 cake tofu, 7.5cm/3in sq. and 2.5cm/1in thick
115g/4oz spinach leaves
750ml/1¼ pints/3 cups vegetable stock
15ml/1 tbsp light soy sauce
salt and ground black pepper

1 Rinse the tofu then cut into 12 small pieces, each about 5mm/¼in thick. Wash the spinach leaves and cut them into small pieces.

2 Pour the vegetable stock into a wok or large, heavy pan and bring to a rolling boil over a medium heat. Add the pieces of tofu and the soy sauce, stir carefully without breaking up the tofu, bring back to the boil, then lower the heat and simmer gently for about 2 minutes.

3 Add the pieces of spinach, and simmer for a further 1–2 minutes. Skim the surface of the soup to remove any foam and to make it clear, then season with salt and ground black pepper to taste. Ladle the soup into warm bowls or a tureen and serve immediately.

Hot-and-sour Soup

This light and invigorating soup is traditionally served at the start of a formal Thai meal.

Serves 4

2 carrots
900ml/1½ pints/3¾ cups vegetable stock
2 Thai chillies, seeded and thinly sliced
2 lemon grass stalks, each cut into 3 pieces
4 kaffir lime leaves
2 garlic cloves, finely chopped
4 spring onions (scallions), thinly sliced
5ml/1 tsp sugar
juice of 1 lime
45ml/3 tbsp chopped fresh coriander (cilantro)
salt
130g/4½ oz/1 cup Japanese tofu, sliced

1 To make carrot flowers, cut each carrot in half crossways, then, using a sharp knife, cut four V-shaped channels lengthways. Slice the carrots into thin rounds and set aside.

COOK'S TIPS
• Kaffir lime leaves have a distinctive citrus flavour. The fresh leaves can be bought from Asian stores, and some supermarkets now sell them dried.
• Before using lemon grass stalks, remove and discard the tough outer layers.
• Thai chillies are notorious for their intense heat, so if you prefer a milder flavour, use only one.

2 Pour the vegetable stock into a large pan. Reserve 2.5ml/½ tsp of the chillies and add the rest to the pan with the lemon grass, lime leaves, garlic and half the spring onions. Bring to the boil, then reduce the heat and simmer for 20 minutes. Strain the stock and discard the flavourings.

3 Return the stock to the pan, add the reserved chillies and spring onions, the sugar, lime juice and coriander and season with salt to taste.

4 Simmer for 5 minutes, then add the carrot flowers and tofu slices, and cook the soup for a further 2 minutes, until the carrot is just tender. Ladle into warm bowls and serve hot.

Chilled Prawn and Cucumber Soup

If you've never served a chilled soup before, this is the one to try first. Delicious and light, it's the perfect way to celebrate summer.

Serves 4

25g/1oz/2 tbsp butter
2 shallots, finely chopped
2 garlic cloves, crushed
1 cucumber, peeled, seeded and diced
300ml/½ pint/1¼ cups milk
225g/8oz cooked peeled prawns (shrimp)
15ml/1 tbsp each finely chopped fresh mint, dill, chives and chervil
300ml/½ pint/1¼ cups whipping cream
salt and ground white pepper

For the garnish
30ml/2 tbsp crème fraîche (optional)
4 large, cooked prawns (shrimp), peeled with tails intact
chopped fresh chives and dill

1 Melt the butter in a pan. Add the shallots and garlic and cook over a low heat, stirring occasionally, for about 4 minutes, until soft but not coloured. Add the cucumber and cook the vegetables gently, stirring frequently, until tender.

2 Stir in the milk, bring almost to the boil, then lower the heat and simmer for 5 minutes. Pour the soup into a blender or food processor and process until very smooth. Season to taste with salt and ground white pepper.

3 Pour the soup into a bowl and set aside to cool. When cool, stir in the prawns, chopped herbs and the whipping cream. Cover the bowl with clear film (plastic wrap) and chill in the refrigerator for at least 2 hours.

4 To serve, ladle the soup into four individual bowls and top each portion with a spoonful of crème fraîche, if using. Place a prawn over the edge of each bowl. Garnish the soup with the chives and dill.

VARIATIONS
• For a change try fresh or canned crab meat or cooked, flaked salmon fillet instead of the prawns.
• If crème fraîche is not available, use sour cream.
• Garnish the soup with a sprinkling of salmon or sea trout roe or, for a truly special occasion, a little caviar.

Malaysian Prawn Laksa

This spicy prawn and noodle stew tastes just as good when made with fresh crab meat or any flaked cooked fish.

Serves 3–4

115g/4oz rice vermicelli or stir-fry rice noodles
15ml/1 tbsp vegetable or groundnut (peanut) oil
600ml/1 pint/2½ cups fish stock
400ml/14fl oz/1⅔ cups thin coconut milk
30ml/2 tbsp Thai fish sauce
½ lime
16–24 cooked peeled prawns (shrimp)
salt and cayenne pepper
60ml/4 tbsp chopped fresh coriander (cilantro), to garnish

For the spicy paste
2 lemon grass stalks, finely chopped
2 fresh red chillies, seeded and chopped
2.5cm/1in piece fresh root ginger, peeled and sliced
2.5ml/½ tsp dried shrimp paste
2 garlic cloves, chopped
2.5ml/½ tsp ground turmeric
30ml/2 tbsp tamarind paste

1 Cook the rice vermicelli or noodles in a large pan of lightly salted, boiling water according to the instructions on the packet. Transfer to a large sieve or colander, then rinse under cold water to stop any further cooking and drain. Set aside and keep warm.

2 To make the spicy paste, place the lemon grass, chillies, ginger, shrimp paste, garlic, turmeric and tamarind paste in a mortar and pound with a pestle until smooth. Alternatively, if you prefer, put all the ingredients in a food processor or blender and then process until a smooth paste is formed.

3 Heat the oil in a large pan, add the spicy paste and cook over a low heat, stirring constantly, for a few moments to release all the flavours, but be careful not to let it burn.

4 Add the fish stock and coconut milk and bring to the boil. Stir in the Thai fish sauce, then simmer for 5 minutes. Season with salt and cayenne to taste, adding a squeeze of lime juice. Add the prawns and heat through gently for a few seconds.

5 Divide the noodles among three or four soup plates. Pour the soup over, making sure that each portion includes an equal number of prawns. Garnish with the chopped coriander and serve piping hot.

Smoked Salmon Pâté

Making this pâté in individual ramekins wrapped in extra smoked salmon gives a really special presentation. Taste the mousse as you are making it as some people prefer more lemon juice.

Serves 4

350g/12oz thinly sliced smoked salmon
150ml/¼ pint/⅔ cup double (heavy) cream
finely grated rind and juice of 1 lemon
salt and ground black pepper
Melba toast, to serve

1 Line four small ramekins with clear film (plastic wrap). Then line the dishes with 115g/4oz of the smoked salmon cut into strips long enough to flop over the edges.

2 In a food processor fitted with a metal blade, process the rest of the salmon with the cream, lemon rind and juice, salt and plenty of pepper.

COOK'S TIP
The quality of smoked salmon is variable. Atlantic salmon is vastly superior to Pacific. Traditional cold smoking over wood still produces the best results.

3 Pack the lined ramekins with the smoked salmon pâté and wrap over the loose strips of salmon. Cover with clear film and chill in the refrigerator for 30 minutes. Invert on to plates and serve with Melba toast.

Smoked Haddock Pâté

The delicate flavour of this pâté makes it the perfect choice for easy entertaining at a light, *al fresco* lunch on a summer's day.

Serves 6

3 large Arbroath smokies, about 225g/8oz each
275g/10oz/1¼ cups medium-fat soft white (farmer's) cheese
3 eggs, beaten
30–45ml/2–3 tbsp lemon juice
ground black pepper
chervil sprigs, to garnish
lemon wedges and lettuce leaves, to serve

1 Preheat the oven to 160°C/325°F/Gas 3. Butter six ramekins.

2 Lay the smokies in an ovenproof dish and heat through in the oven for 10 minutes. Carefully remove the skin and bones from the smokies, then flake the flesh into a bowl.

3 Mash the fish with a fork and work in the cheese, then the eggs. Add lemon juice and pepper to taste.

COOK'S TIP
Arbroath smokies, also known as Aberdeen smokies, are small haddock that have been gutted and had their heads removed before being hot smoked over peat. They are a Scottish speciality, but if they are not available, substitute with traditionally smoked haddock.

4 Divide the fish mixture among the ramekins and place in a large-sized roasting pan. Pour hot water into the roasting pan to come halfway up the side of the ramekins. Bake for 30 minutes, until just set.

5 Leave to cool for 2–3 minutes, then run the point of a knife around the edge of each dish and invert on to a warmed plate. Garnish with chervil sprigs and serve with the lemon wedges and lettuce.

Chicken Liver Pâté with Garlic

This smooth pâté is indulgent and absolutely delicious. Start preparation the day before so that the flavour can develop fully.

Serves 6–8

225g/8oz/1 cup unsalted (sweet) butter
400g/14oz chicken livers, chopped
45–60ml/3–4 tbsp Madeira
3 large shallots, chopped
2 large garlic cloves, finely chopped
5ml/1 tsp finely chopped fresh thyme
pinch of ground allspice
30ml/2 tbsp double (heavy) cream (optional)
salt and ground black pepper
small fresh bay leaves or fresh thyme sprigs, to garnish
toast and small pickled gherkins, to serve

1 Melt 75g/3oz/6 tbsp butter in a small pan over a low heat, then leave it to bubble gently until it is clear. Pour off the clarified butter into a bowl.

2 Melt 40g/1½oz/3 tbsp butter in a frying pan and cook the chicken livers for 4–5 minutes, or until browned. Stir frequently to make sure that the livers cook evenly. Do not overcook them or they will be tough.

3 Add 45ml/3 tbsp Madeira and set it alight, then scrape the contents of the pan into a food processor or blender.

4 Melt 25g/1oz/2 tbsp butter in the pan over a low heat and cook the shallots for 5 minutes, or until soft. Add the garlic, thyme and allspice and cook for another 2–3 minutes. Add this mixture to the livers with the remaining butter and cream, if using, then process until smooth.

5 Add about 7.5ml/1½ tsp each of salt and black pepper and more Madeira to taste. Scrape the pâté into a serving dish and place a few bay leaves or thyme sprigs on top. Melt the clarified butter, if necessary, then pour it over the pâté. Cool and chill the pâté for 4 hours or overnight.

VARIATIONS
• Cognac, Armagnac or port can be used instead of Madeira.
• Use duck livers instead of chicken and add 2.5ml/½ tsp grated orange rind.
• Use chopped fresh tarragon instead of the thyme.

Herbed Liver Pâté Pie

Serve this highly flavoured pâté with a glass of Pilsner beer for a change from wine.

Serves 10

675g/1½ lb minced (ground) pork
350g/12oz pork liver
350g/12oz/2 cups diced cooked ham
1 small onion, finely chopped
30ml/2 tbsp chopped fresh parsley
5ml/1 tsp German mustard
30ml/2 tbsp Kirsch
5ml/1 tsp salt
beaten egg, for sealing and glazing
25g/1oz sachet (envelope) aspic jelly
250ml/8fl oz/1 cup boiling water
ground black pepper
mustard, crusty bread and dill pickles, to serve

For the pastry
450g/1lb/4 cups plain (all-purpose) flour
pinch of salt
275g/10oz/1¼ cups butter
2 eggs plus 1 egg yolk
30ml/2 tbsp water

1 Preheat the oven to 200°C/400°F/Gas 6. To make the pastry, sift the flour and salt and rub in the butter. Beat the eggs, egg yolk and water, add to the dry ingredients and mix.

2 Knead the dough briefly until smooth. Roll out two-thirds on a lightly floured surface and use to line a 10 x 25cm/4 x 10in hinged loaf tin (pan). Trim any excess dough.

3 Process half the pork and all of the liver until fairly smooth. Stir in the remaining minced pork, ham, onion, parsley, mustard, Kirsch, salt and black pepper to taste.

4 Spoon the filling into the tin and level the surface.

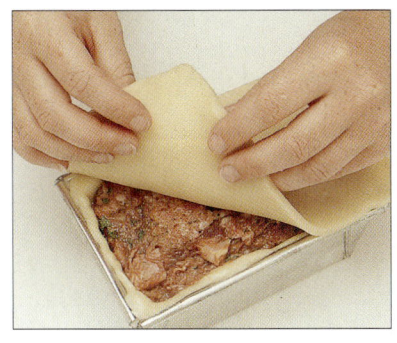

5 Roll out the remaining pastry on the lightly floured surface and use it to top the pie, brushing the edges with some of the beaten egg to seal. Decorate with the pastry trimmings and brush with the remaining beaten egg to glaze. Using a fork, make three or four holes in the top, for the steam to escape during cooking.

6 Bake for 40 minutes, then reduce the oven temperature to 180°C/350°F/Gas 4 and cook for a further hour. Cover the pastry with foil if the top begins to brown too much. Leave the pie to cool in the tin.

7 Make up the aspic jelly, using the boiling water or according to the packet instructions. Stir to dissolve, then leave to cool.

8 Make a small hole near the edge of the pie with a skewer, then pour in the aspic through a greaseproof paper funnel. Chill in the refrigerator for at least 2 hours before slicing and serving the pie with mustard, crusty bread and dill pickles.

Prawn, Egg and Avocado Mousses

A light and creamy mousse with lots of chunky texture and a great mix of flavours.

Serves 6

a little olive oil
juice and rind of 1 lemon
1 sachet gelatine
60ml/4 tbsp good-quality mayonnaise
60ml/4 tbsp chopped fresh dill
5ml/1 tsp anchovy essence (extract)
5ml/1 tsp Worcestershire sauce
1 large avocado, ripe but just firm
4 hard-boiled eggs, shelled and chopped
175g/6oz/1 cup cooked peeled prawns (shrimp), coarsely chopped if large
250ml/8fl oz/1 cup double (heavy) or whipping cream, lightly whipped
2 egg whites, whisked
salt and ground black pepper
fresh dill or parsley sprigs, to garnish
warm bread or toast, to serve

1 Prepare six small ramekins. Lightly grease the dishes with olive oil, then wrap a greaseproof (waxed) paper collar around the top of each and secure with tape. This makes sure that you can fill the dishes as high as you like, and the extra mixture will be supported while it is setting. The mousses will look really dramatic when you remove the paper. Alternatively, prepare just one medium soufflé dish.

2 Put the lemon juice into a small, heatproof bowl, stir in 15ml/1 tbsp hot water and sprinkle over the gelatine. Leave for 5 minutes, until spongy, then set the bowl over hot water, until clear, stirring occasionally. Leave to cool slightly, then blend in the lemon rind, mayonnaise, dill, anchovy essence and Worcestershire sauce.

3 Cut the avocado in half, twist to separate and remove the stone (pit) with the point of the knife. In a medium bowl mash the avocado flesh, then mix in the eggs and prawns. Stir in the gelatine mixture and then fold in the cream and egg whites. Season to taste with salt and pepper. When evenly blended, spoon into the ramekins or soufflé dish and chill for 3–4 hours.

4 Garnish with the dill or parsley and serve the mousse with bread or toast.

COOK'S TIP
Other fish can make a good alternative to prawns (shrimp). Try substituting the same quantity of smoked trout or salmon, or cooked crab meat.

Sea Trout Mousse

This deliciously creamy mousse makes a little sea trout go a long way. It is equally good made with salmon if sea trout is unavailable. Serve with crisp Melba toast or triangles of lightly toasted pitta bread.

Serves 6

250g/9oz sea trout fillet
120ml/4fl oz/½ cup fish stock
2 gelatine leaves, or 15ml/1 tbsp
   powdered gelatine
juice of ½ lemon
30ml/2 tbsp dry sherry or dry vermouth
30ml/2 tbsp freshly grated Parmesan
300ml/½ pint/1¼ cups whipping cream
2 egg whites
15ml/1 tbsp sunflower oil, for greasing
salt and ground white pepper

For the garnish
5cm/2in piece cucumber, with peel,
   thinly sliced and halved
fresh dill or chervil

1 Put the sea trout in a large, shallow pan. Pour in the fish stock and heat gently to simmering point. Poach the fish for about 3–4 minutes, until it is lightly cooked. Carefully strain the stock into a jug (pitcher) and leave the sea trout to cool slightly.

2 Add the gelatine to the reserved hot stock and stir well until it has dissolved completely. Cover and set aside until required.

3 When the sea trout is cool enough to handle, remove and discard the skin and any stray bones, then flake the flesh. Pour the stock into a food processor or blender. Process briefly, then gradually add the flaked sea trout, lemon juice, sherry or vermouth and Parmesan through the feeder tube, continuing to process the mixture until it is smooth. Scrape into a large bowl and leave to cool completely.

4 Lightly whip the cream in a bowl, then fold it into the cold trout mixture. Season to taste with salt and pepper, then cover with clear film (plastic wrap) and chill until the mousse is just starting to set. It should have the consistency of mayonnaise.

5 In a clean, grease-free bowl, beat the egg whites with a pinch of salt until they form soft peaks. Then using a large metal spoon or rubber spatula, stir about one-third of the egg whites into the sea trout mixture to slacken it slightly, then carefully fold in the remainder.

6 Lightly grease six ramekins or similar individual serving dishes. Divide the mousse equally among the prepared dishes and level the surface. Place in the refrigerator for 2–3 hours, until set. Just before serving, arrange a few slices of cucumber and a small herb sprig on top of each mousse and, finally, sprinkle over a little chopped dill or chervil.

Grilled Vegetable Terrine

A colourful, layered terrine, this dish uses all the vegetables that are associated with the Mediterranean.

Serves 6

2 large red (bell) peppers, quartered and seeded
2 large yellow (bell) peppers, quartered and seeded
1 large aubergine (eggplant), sliced lengthways
2 large courgettes (zucchini), sliced lengthways
90ml/6 tbsp olive oil
1 large red onion, thinly sliced
75g/3oz/½ cup raisins
15ml/1 tbsp tomato purée (paste)
15ml/1 tbsp red wine vinegar
400ml/14fl oz/1⅔ cups tomato juice
30ml/2 tbsp powdered gelatine
fresh basil leaves, to garnish

For the dressing
90ml/6 tbsp extra virgin olive oil
30ml/2 tbsp red wine vinegar
salt and ground black pepper

1 Place the peppers skin side up under a hot grill (broiler) and cook until the skins are blackened. Transfer to a bowl and cover with a plate. Leave to cool.

2 Arrange the slices of aubergine and courgette on separate baking sheets. Brush them with a little olive oil and cook under the grill, turning them occasionally, until they are tender and golden brown.

3 Heat the remaining olive oil in a frying pan and add the sliced onion, raisins, tomato purée and red wine vinegar. Cook over a low heat, stirring occasionally, until the mixture is soft and syrupy. Set aside and leave to cool in the frying pan.

4 Line a 1.75 litre/3 pint/7½ cup terrine with clear film (plastic wrap). It helps if you lightly oil the terrine first. Leave a little clear film overhanging the sides of the container.

5 Pour half the tomato juice into a pan and sprinkle with the gelatine. Leave for 5 minutes to soften, then dissolve gently over a low heat, stirring to prevent any lumps from forming.

6 Place a layer of the grilled (broiled) red peppers in the base of the terrine and pour in enough of the tomato juice with gelatine to cover it.

COOK'S TIP
If you don't own a terrine, you can use a loaf tin (pan) instead. It will still need to be lined with clear film (plastic wrap).

7 Continue layering the vegetables, pouring tomato juice over each layer, finishing with a layer of red peppers. Add the remaining tomato juice to the pan and pour into the terrine. Give it a sharp tap, to disperse the juice. Cover and chill until set.

8 To make the dressing, whisk together the oil and vinegar, then season to taste. Turn out the terrine and remove the clear film. Serve in thick slices, drizzled with dressing and garnished with basil leaves.

VARIATION
Use orange and green peppers along with or in place of the red and yellow ones. Green beans, simply boiled first, would make a tasty addition, as would a colourful layer of peas or corn.

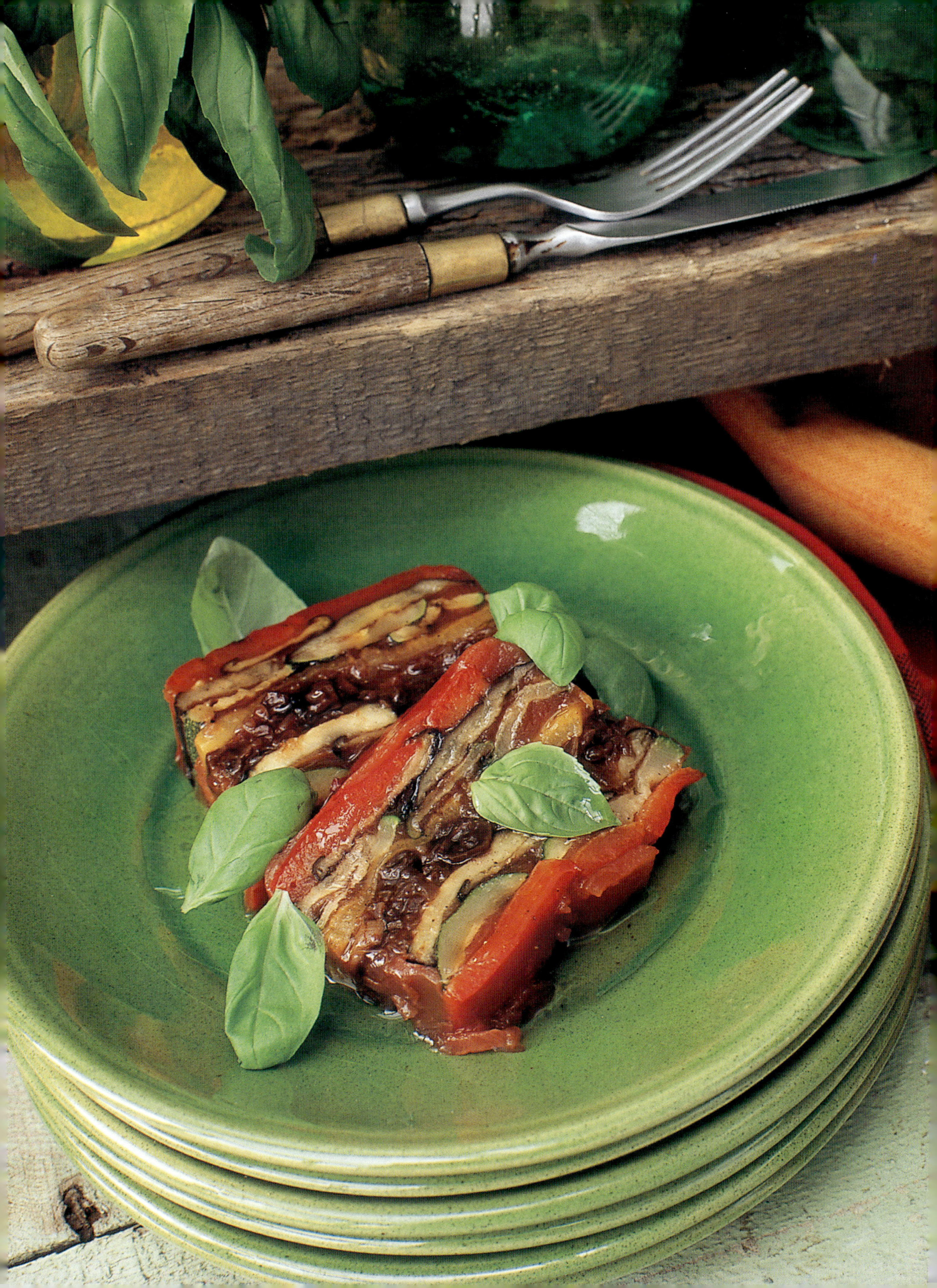

Roast Pepper Terrine

This terrine is perfect for all kinds of entertaining because it tastes better if made ahead. Prepare the salsa on the day of serving. Serve with Italian bread.

Serves 8

8 (bell) peppers (red, yellow
   and orange)
675g/1½lb/3 cups mascarpone cheese
3 eggs, separated
30ml/2 tbsp each coarsely chopped
   flat leaf parsley and shredded basil
2 large garlic cloves, coarsely chopped
2 red, yellow or orange (bell) peppers,
   seeded and coarsely chopped
30ml/2 tbsp extra virgin olive oil
10ml/2 tsp balsamic vinegar
a few fresh basil sprigs
salt and ground black pepper

1 Place the whole peppers under a hot grill (broiler) for 8–10 minutes, turning them frequently, until blackened and charred. Then put into a plastic bag, tie the top and leave until cold before peeling and seeding them. Slice seven of the peppers lengthways into thin strips and reserve the eighth.

2 Put the mascarpone cheese in a bowl with the egg yolks, parsley, basil and half the garlic. Season with salt and pepper to taste. Beat well. In a separate, grease-free bowl, whisk the egg whites to a soft peak, then fold into the cheese mixture until they are evenly incorporated.

3 Preheat the oven to 180°C/350°F/Gas 4. Line the base of a lightly oiled 900g/2lb loaf tin (pan). Put one-third of the cheese mixture in the tin and spread evenly, levelling the surface. Arrange half the pepper strips on top in an even layer. Repeat until all the cheese and pepper strips have been used, ending with a layer of the mascarpone cheese mixture.

4 Cover the tin with foil and place in a roasting pan. Pour in boiling water to come halfway up the sides of the loaf tin. Bake for 1 hour. Remove from the oven and leave the terrine to cool in the water bath, then lift out and chill overnight in the refrigerator.

5 A few hours before serving, make the salsa. Place the remaining peeled pepper and fresh peppers in a food processor. Add the remaining garlic, oil and vinegar. Set aside a few basil leaves for garnishing and add the rest to the processor. Process until finely chopped. Tip the mixture into a bowl, season with salt and pepper to taste and mix well. Cover with clear film (plastic wrap) and chill in the refrigerator until ready to serve.

6 Turn out the terrine on to a chopping board, peel off the lining paper and slice thickly. Garnish with the reserved basil leaves and serve cold, with the sweet pepper salsa.

Asparagus and Egg Terrine

For a special occasion, this terrine is a delicious choice yet it is very light. Make the hollandaise sauce well in advance and warm through gently when required.

Serves 8

150ml/¼ pint/⅔ cup milk
150ml/¼ pint/⅔ cup double (heavy) cream
40g/1½oz/3 tbsp butter
40g/1½oz/3 tbsp plain (all-purpose) flour
75g/3oz herbed or garlic cream cheese
675g/1½ lb asparagus spears, cooked
vegetable oil, for brushing
2 eggs, separated
15ml/1 tbsp chopped fresh chives
30ml/2 tbsp chopped fresh dill
salt and ground black pepper
fresh dill sprigs, to garnish

For the orange hollandaise sauce
15ml/1 tbsp white wine vinegar
15ml/1 tbsp fresh orange juice
4 black peppercorns
1 bay leaf
2 egg yolks
115g/4oz/½ cup butter, melted and cooled slightly

1 Put the milk and cream into a small pan and heat to just below boiling point. Melt the butter in a medium pan, stir in the flour and cook over a low heat, stirring constantly, to a thick paste. Gradually stir in the milk, whisking as it thickens. Stir in the cream cheese, season to taste with salt and ground black pepper and leave to cool slightly.

2 Trim the asparagus to fit the width of a 1.2 litre/2 pint/5 cup loaf tin (pan) or terrine. Lightly oil the tin and then base line with baking parchment. Preheat the oven to 180°C/350°F/Gas 4.

3 Beat the egg yolks into the sauce mixture. Whisk the whites until stiff and fold in with the chives, dill and seasoning. Layer the asparagus and egg mixture in the tin, starting and finishing with asparagus. Cover the top with foil.

4 Place the terrine in a roasting pan and half fill with hot water. Cook for 45–55 minutes, until firm.

5 When the terrine is just firm to the touch, remove from the oven and leave to cool, then chill.

6 To make the sauce, put the vinegar, orange juice, peppercorns and bay leaf in a small pan and heat gently until reduced by half.

7 Cool the sauce slightly, then whisk in the egg yolks, then the butter, with a balloon whisk over a very gentle heat. Season to taste with salt and pepper and continue whisking until thick. Keep the sauce warm over a pan of hot water.

8 Invert the terrine on to a serving dish, remove the paper and garnish with the dill. Cut into slices and pour over the warmed sauce.

Haddock and Smoked Salmon Terrine

This is a fairly substantial terrine, so serve modest slices, perhaps accompanied by fresh dill mayonnaise or a fresh mango salsa. It would be perfect for a summer lunch party.

Serves 10–12

15ml/1 tbsp sunflower oil, for greasing
350g/12oz thinly sliced oak-smoked salmon
900g/2lb haddock fillets
2 eggs, lightly beaten
105ml/7 tbsp crème fraîche
30ml/2 tbsp drained capers
30ml/2 tbsp drained soft green or pink peppercorns
salt and ground white pepper
crème fraîche, peppercorns and fresh dill and rocket (arugula), to garnish

1 Preheat the oven to 200°C/400°F/Gas 6. Grease a 1 litre/1¾ pint/4 cup loaf tin (pan) or terrine with the sunflower oil. Use some of the smoked salmon slices to line the loaf tin or terrine, allowing the ends to overhang the rim of the mould slightly. Set aside the remaining smoked salmon until it is needed.

2 Skin the haddock fillets. Using a sharp knife, cut two long slices of haddock the same length as the loaf tin or terrine and set aside. Cut the remaining haddock fillets into small pieces. Season all of the haddock with salt and ground white pepper.

3 Combine the eggs, crème fraîche, capers and green or pink peppercorns in a bowl. Add salt and pepper and stir in the haddock pieces. Spoon the mixture into the mould until it is about one-third full. Smooth the surface with a spatula.

4 Wrap the long haddock slices in the reserved smoked salmon. Lay them on top of the layer of the fish mixture in the tin or terrine.

5 Cover with the rest of the fish mixture, smooth the surface and fold the overhanging pieces of smoked salmon over the top. Cover tightly with a double thickness of foil. Tap the terrine to settle the contents.

6 Stand the loaf tin or terrine in a roasting pan and pour in boiling water to come halfway up the sides of the tin or terrine. Place in the oven and cook for 45 minutes–1 hour, until the filling is just set.

7 Take the terrine out of the water bath, but do not remove the foil cover. Place two or three large heavy cans on the foil to weigh it and leave until cold. Chill in the refrigerator for 24 hours.

8 About an hour before serving, remove the terrine from the refrigerator, lift off the weights and remove the foil. Carefully invert on to a serving plate and garnish with crème fraîche, peppercorns and sprigs of dill and rocket leaves.

COOK'S TIP
If you are going to slice a side of salmon yourself, you will need a very sharp knife with a thin 25cm/10in blade.

VARIATION
Use any thick white fish fillets for this terrine. Try cod, whiting, hake, or hoki.

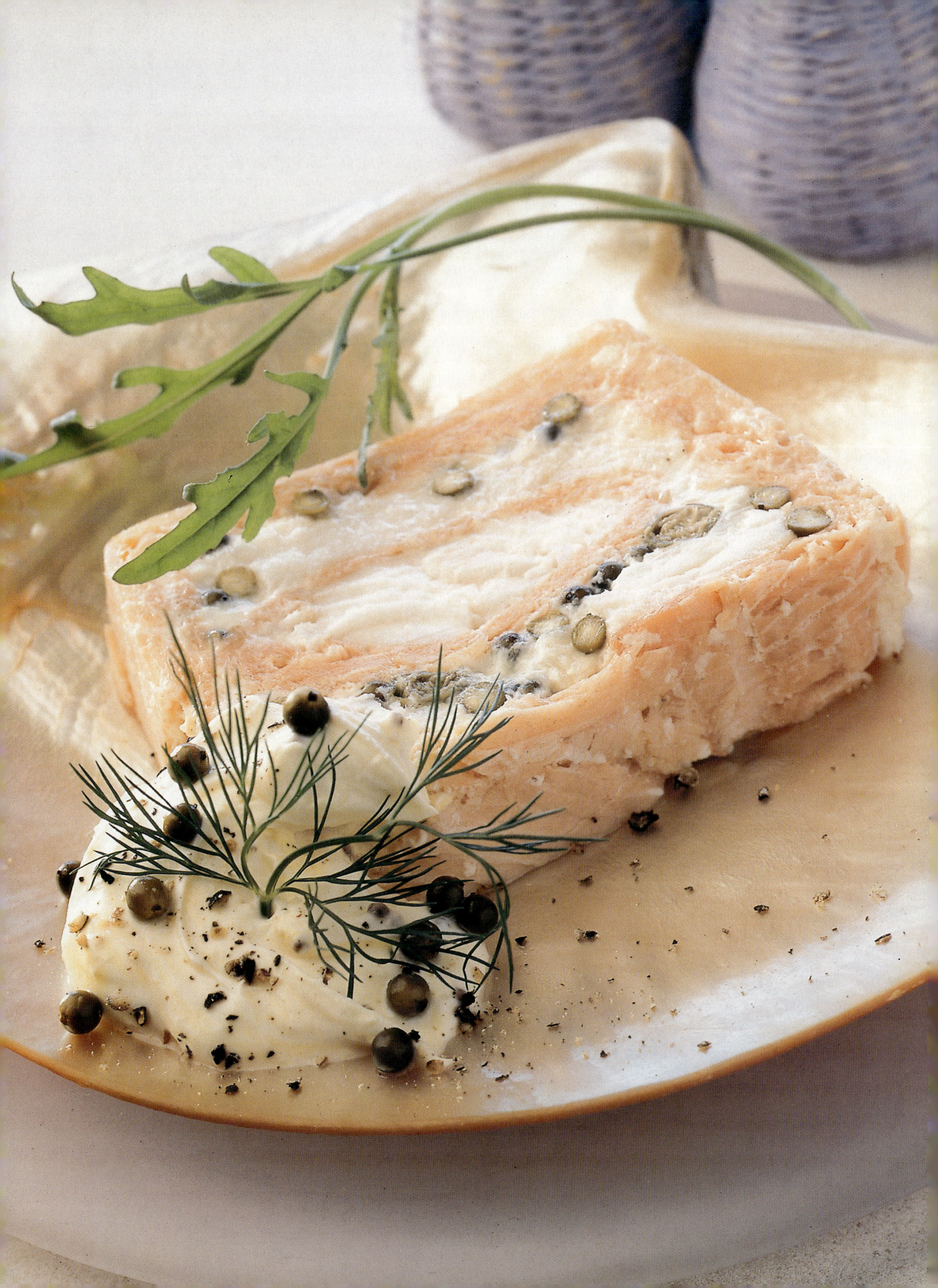

Hot Crab Soufflés

These delicious little soufflés must be served as soon as they are ready, so seat your guests at the table before taking the soufflés out of the oven.

Serves 6

50g/2oz/¼ cup butter
45ml/3 tbsp fine wholemeal (whole-wheat) breadcrumbs
4 spring onions (scallions), finely chopped
15ml/1 tbsp Malayan or mild Madras curry powder
25g/1oz/2 tbsp plain (all-purpose) flour
105ml/7 tbsp coconut milk or milk
150ml/¼ pint/⅔ cup whipping cream
4 egg yolks
225g/8oz white crab meat
mild green Tabasco sauce
6 egg whites
salt and ground black pepper

1 Use some of the butter to grease six ramekins or a 1.75 litre/3 pint/7½ cup soufflé dish. Sprinkle the breadcrumbs in the dishes or dish and roll them around to coat the base and sides completely, then tip out the excess breadcrumbs. Preheat the oven to 200°C/400°F/Gas 6.

2 Melt the remaining butter in a pan, add the spring onions and Malayan or mild Madras curry powder and cook over a low heat, stirring frequently, for about 1 minute, until softened. Stir in the flour and cook, stirring constantly, for 1 minute more.

3 Gradually add the coconut milk or milk and the cream, stirring constantly. Cook over a low heat, still stirring, until smooth and thick. Remove the pan from the heat, stir in the egg yolks, then the crab. Season to taste with salt, black pepper and Tabasco sauce.

4 In a clean grease-free bowl, whisk the egg whites with a pinch of salt until they are stiff. Using a metal spoon, stir one-third of the whites into the crab mixture to slacken, then fold in the remainder. Spoon into the dishes or dish.

5 Bake the soufflés until well risen, golden brown and just firm to the touch. Individual soufflés will take about 8 minutes, while a large, single soufflé will take 15–20 minutes. Serve immediately.

Twice-baked Gruyère and Potato Soufflés

This recipe can be prepared in advance and given its second baking just before you serve it up.

Serves 4

225g/8oz floury (mealy) potatoes
2 eggs, separated
175g/6oz/1½ cups grated Gruyère cheese
50g/2oz/½ cup self-raising (self-rising) flour
50g/2oz spinach leaves
butter, for greasing
salt and ground black pepper

1 Preheat the oven to 200°C/400°F/Gas 6. Peel the potatoes and cook in lightly salted, boiling water for 20 minutes, until very tender. Drain well and mash with the egg yolks, using a potato masher or a fork.

2 Stir in half of the Gruyère cheese and all of the flour. Season to taste with salt and ground black pepper.

COOK'S TIP
Never attempt to mash potatoes with an electric mixer. It breaks down the starch and turns the potatoes into a sticky mess with the texture of wallpaper paste. Use a potato masher or fork to pound them by hand or a potato ricer which will produce an even, lump-free, fine mash.

3 Finely chop the spinach and fold into the potato mixture.

VARIATION
Try replacing the Gruyère with a crumbled blue cheese, such as Stilton or Shropshire Blue, which have a stronger flavour.

4 Whisk the egg whites in a clean, grease-free bowl until they form soft peaks. Fold a little of the egg white into the mixture to slacken it slightly, then, using a large spoon, fold the remaining egg white into the mixture.

5 Grease four large ramekins. Pour the mixture into the dishes and place on a baking sheet. Bake for 20 minutes. Remove the dishes from the oven and leave to cool.

6 Turn the soufflés out on to a baking sheet and sprinkle with the remaining cheese. Bake again for 5 minutes and serve immediately.

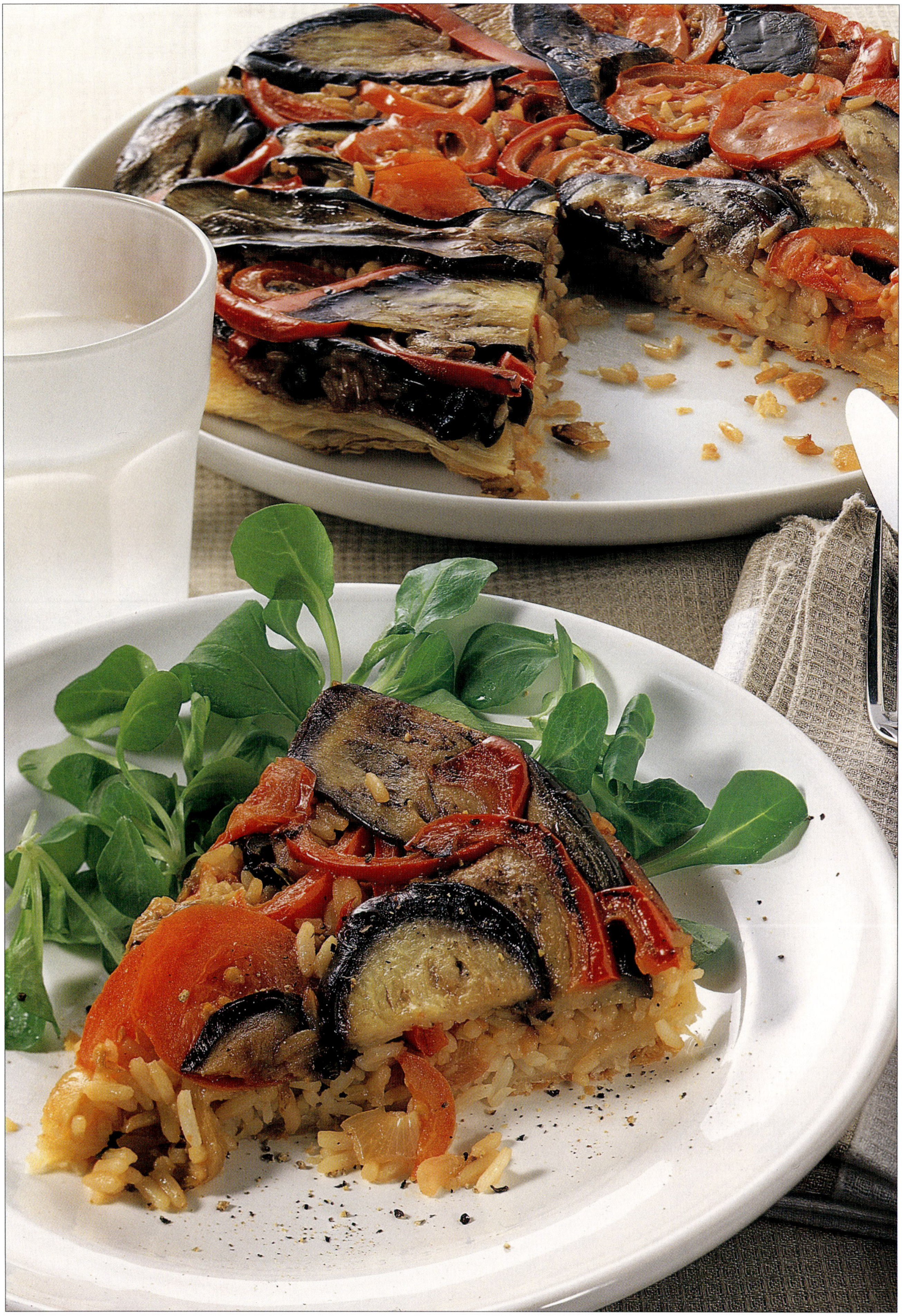

Pastries, Tartlets & Toasts

Nothing compares with the taste of home-made, buttery pastry; few things are as impressive as a dainty filo pastry cup filled with prawns, or a simple and elegant appetizer of cannellini beans and fruity olive oil on crispy bruschetta.

Garlic Prawns in Filo Tartlets

Tartlets made with crisp layers of filo pastry and filled with garlic prawns make a tempting appetizer.

Serves 4

50g/2oz/4 tbsp butter, melted
2–3 large sheets filo pastry

For the filling
115g/4oz/½ cup butter
2–3 garlic cloves, crushed
1 fresh red chilli, seeded and chopped
350g/12oz/3 cups cooked peeled prawns (shrimp)
30ml/2 tbsp chopped fresh parsley or fresh chives
salt and ground black pepper

1 Preheat the oven to 200°C/400°F/Gas 6. Brush four 7.5cm/3in flan tins (quiche pans) with melted butter.

2 Cut the filo pastry into twelve 10cm/4in squares and brush them with the melted butter.

3 Place three squares inside each tin, overlapping them at slight angles and frilling the edges and points while forming a good hollow in each centre.

4 Bake for 10–15 minutes, until crisp and golden. Leave to cool slightly, then remove the pastry cases (pie shells) from the tins.

5 Meanwhile, make the filling. Melt the butter in a large frying pan, then add the garlic, chilli and prawns and cook quickly for 1–2 minutes to warm through. Stir in the fresh parsley or chives and season with salt and plenty of black pepper.

6 Spoon the prawn filling into the tartlets and serve immediately, perhaps with some sour cream.

Crab and Ricotta Tartlets

Use the meat from a freshly cooked crab, weighing about 450g/1lb, if you can. Otherwise, look out for frozen brown and white crab meat.

Serves 4

225g/8oz/2 cups plain (all-purpose) flour
pinch of salt
115g/4oz/½ cup butter, diced
225g/8oz/1 cup ricotta cheese
15ml/1 tbsp grated onion
30ml/2 tbsp freshly grated Parmesan cheese
2.5ml/½ tsp mustard powder
2 eggs, plus 1 egg yolk
225g/8oz crab meat
30ml/2 tbsp chopped fresh parsley
2.5–5ml/½–1 tsp anchovy essence (extract)
5–10ml/1–2 tsp lemon juice
salt and cayenne pepper
salad leaves, to garnish

1 Sift the flour and salt into a bowl, add the butter and rub it in until the mixture resembles fine breadcrumbs. Stir in about 60ml/4 tbsp cold water to make a firm dough.

2 Turn the dough on to a lightly-floured surface and knead lightly. Roll out the pastry and use to line four 10cm/4in tartlet tins (muffin pans). Prick the bases all over with a fork, then chill in the refrigerator for about 30 minutes. Preheat the oven to 200°C/400°F/Gas 6.

3 Line the pastry cases (pie shells) with baking parchment or foil and fill with baking beans. Bake them for 10 minutes, then remove the paper or foil and beans. Return to the oven and bake for a further 10 minutes.

4 Place the ricotta, grated onion, Parmesan and mustard powder in a bowl and beat until soft and well combined. Gradually beat in the eggs and egg yolk.

5 Gently stir in the crab meat and chopped parsley, then add the anchovy essence and lemon juice and season with salt and cayenne pepper, to taste.

6 Remove the tartlet cases from the oven and reduce the temperature to 180°C/350°F/Gas 4. Spoon the filling evenly into the cases and bake for 20 minutes, until set and golden brown. Serve hot with a garnish of salad leaves.

Tiger Prawns with Mint, Dill and Lime

A wonderful combination – mint, dill and lime blend together to make a magical concoction to flavour succulent tiger prawns that will delight everyone who tries it.

Serves 4

4 large sheets filo pastry
75g/3oz/1/3 cup butter
16 large tiger prawns (jumbo shrimp), cooked and peeled
15ml/1 tbsp chopped fresh mint, plus extra to garnish
15ml/1 tbsp chopped fresh dill
juice of 1 lime
8 cooked unpeeled tiger prawns (jumbo shrimp) and lime wedges, to serve

1 Keep the sheets of filo pastry covered with a dry, clean dishtowel to keep them moist. Melt the butter in a small pan over a low heat, then remove the pan from the heat. Cut one sheet of filo pastry in half widthways and brush with some of the melted butter. Place one half on top of the other.

2 Preheat the oven to 230°C/450°F/Gas 8. Cut the tiger prawns in half down the back of the prawn and remove the dark vein.

3 Place four prawns in the centre of the double layer of filo pastry and sprinkle a quarter of the mint, dill and lime juice over the top. Fold over the sides, brush with butter and roll up to make a parcel.

4 Make three more parcels in the same way. Place all the parcels, join side down, on a lightly greased baking sheet. Bake for 10 minutes, or until golden. Serve immediately, garnished with whole tiger prawns, lime wedges and extra chopped mint.

Wild Mushroom and Fontina Tarts

Italian fontina cheese gives these tarts a creamy, nutty flavour.

Serves 4

25g/1oz/½ cup dried wild mushrooms
1 red onion, chopped
30ml/2 tbsp olive oil
2 garlic cloves, chopped
30ml/2 tbsp medium-dry sherry
1 egg
120ml/4fl oz/½ cup single (light) cream
25g/1oz fontina cheese, thinly sliced
salt and ground black pepper
rocket (arugula) leaves, to serve

For the pastry
115g/4oz/1 cup wholemeal (whole-wheat) flour
50g/2oz/4 tbsp unsalted (sweet) butter
25g/1oz/¼ cup walnuts, roasted and ground
1 egg, lightly beaten

1 To make the pastry, sift the flour into a bowl and rub in butter with your fingertips until the mixture resembles fine breadcrumbs. Add the nuts then the egg and mix to a soft dough. Gather into a ball, wrap, then chill for 30 minutes.

2 Meanwhile, place the dried wild mushrooms in a bowl and add 300ml/½ pint/1¼ cups boiling water. Soak for 30 minutes. Drain well and reserve the liquid. Cook the onion in the oil for 5 minutes, then add the garlic and cook for about 2 minutes, stirring.

3 Add the soaked mushrooms and cook for 7 minutes over a high heat until the edges become crisp. Add the sherry and the reserved mushroom soaking liquid. Cook over a high heat for about 10 minutes, until the liquid has evaporated. Season to taste with salt and pepper and set aside to cool.

COOK'S TIPS
• You can prepare the pastry cases (pie shells) in advance, bake them blind for 10 minutes, then store in an airtight container for up to 2 days.
• Baking beans are small metal weights that help to prevent the pastry case from shrinking and blistering during the initial baking. You can, of course, use real dried beans that are kept especially for the purpose.

4 Preheat the oven to 200°C/400°F/Gas 6. Lightly grease four 10cm/4in tartlet tins (muffin pans). Roll out the pastry on a lightly floured work surface and use to line the tart tins.

5 Prick the pastry bases all over with a fork, line with baking parchment and baking beans and bake blind for about 10 minutes. Remove the paper and the beans.

6 Whisk the egg and cream to mix, add to the mushroom mixture, then season to taste with salt and pepper. Spoon the filling into the pastry cases (pie shells), top with cheese slices and bake for 15–20 minutes, until the filling is set. Leave to cool slightly, then serve warm with rocket.

Vegetable Tarte Tatin

This upside-down tart combines Mediterranean vegetables with rice, garlic, onions and olives.

Serves 4

30ml/2 tbsp sunflower oil
25ml/1½ tbsp olive oil
1 aubergine (eggplant), sliced lengthways
1 large red (bell) pepper, seeded and cut into long strips
5 tomatoes
2 red shallots, finely chopped
1–2 garlic cloves, crushed
150ml/¼ pint/⅔ cup white wine
10ml/2 tsp chopped fresh basil
225g/8oz/2 cups cooked rice
40g/1½oz/⅔ cup pitted black olives, chopped
350g/12oz puff pastry, thawed if frozen
ground black pepper
salad leaves, to serve

1 Preheat the oven to 190°C/375°F/Gas 5. Heat the sunflower oil with 15ml/1 tbsp of the olive oil. Add the aubergine slices and cook over a medium heat for 4–5 minutes on each side. Drain on kitchen paper.

COOK'S TIP
Modern varieties of aubergine no longer contain bitter juices that must be removed before cooking by salting. However, if you have time, it is still worth doing this because it helps to prevent them from soaking up large amounts of oil during cooking.

2 Add the pepper strips to the oil remaining in the pan, turning them to coat. Cover the pan with a lid or a sheet of foil and sweat the peppers over a moderately high heat for 5–6 minutes, stirring occasionally, until the pepper strips are soft and flecked with brown.

3 Slice two of the tomatoes and set them aside. Place the remaining tomatoes in a bowl, cover with boiling water and leave for 30 seconds, then drain and peel them. Cut them into quarters and remove the cores and seeds. Chop the tomato flesh coarsely.

4 Heat the remaining oil in the frying pan. Add the shallots and garlic and cook over a low heat, stirring occasionally, for 3–4 minutes, until softened but not browned. Then add the chopped tomatoes and cook, for a few minutes, until just softened. Stir in the white wine and basil and season with black pepper to taste. Bring to the boil, then remove the pan from the heat and stir in the cooked rice and black olives.

5 Arrange the tomato slices, the aubergine slices and the peppers in a single layer on the base of a heavy, 30cm/12in, shallow ovenproof dish. Spread the rice and tomato mixture evenly on top.

6 Roll out the pastry to a round slightly larger than the diameter of the dish and place on top of the rice, gently tucking the overlap down inside the dish.

7 Bake for 25–30 minutes, until the pastry is golden and risen. Leave to cool slightly, then invert the tart on to a large, warmed serving plate. Serve in slices, with some salad leaves.

VARIATION
Courgettes (zucchini) and mushrooms could be used as well as, or instead of, the aubergines and pepper. Alternatively, you could use strips of lightly browned chicken.

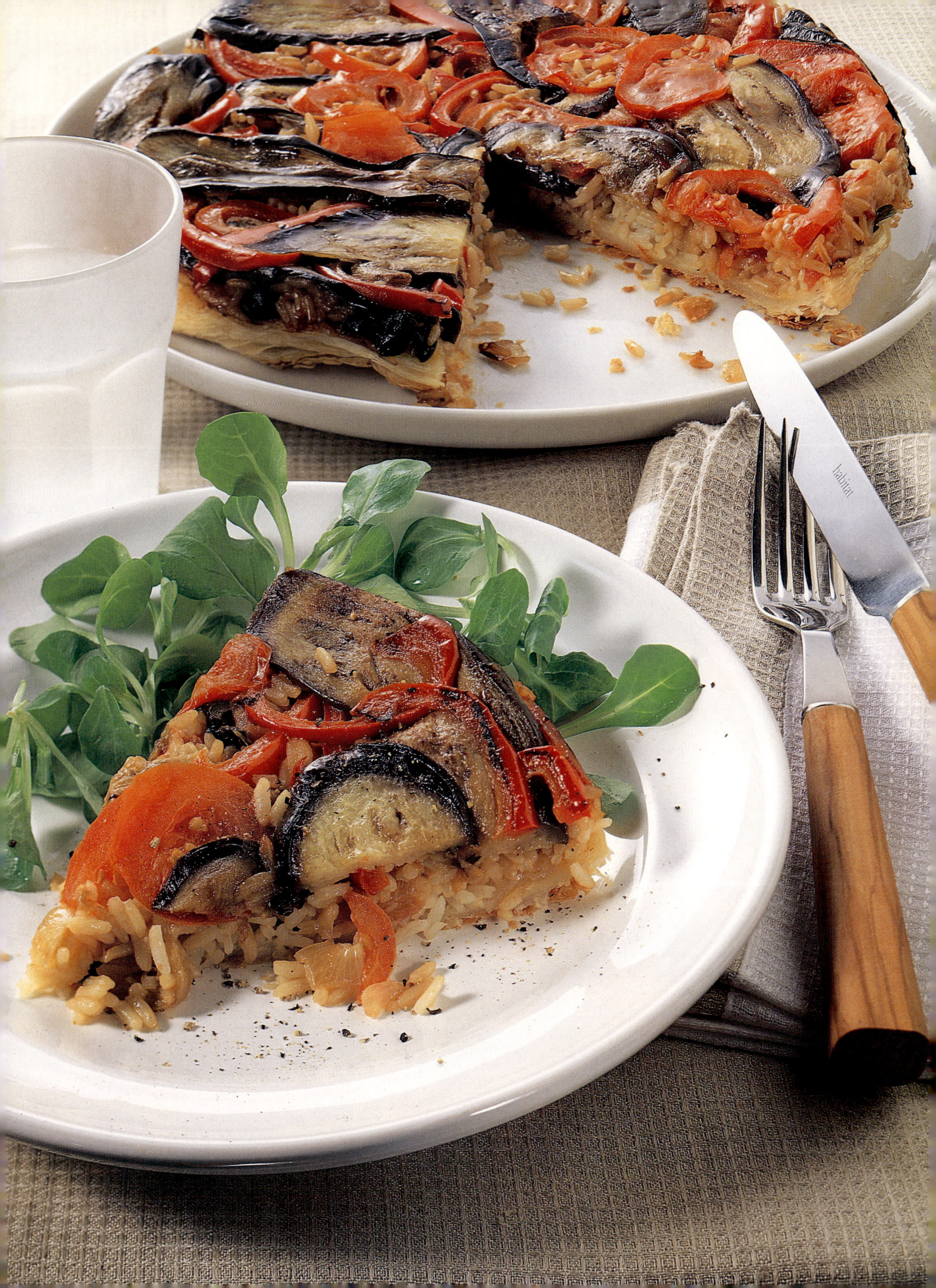
habitat

Greek Aubergine and Spinach Pie

Aubergines layered with spinach, feta cheese and rice make a flavoursome and dramatic filling for a pie. It can be served warm or cold in elegant slices.

Serves 12

375g/13oz shortcrust pastry, thawed if frozen
45–60ml/3–4 tbsp olive oil
1 large aubergine (eggplant), sliced into rounds
1 onion, chopped
1 garlic clove, crushed
175g/6oz spinach
4 eggs
75g/3oz/1/2 cup crumbled feta cheese
40g/1 1/2oz/1/2 cup freshly grated Parmesan cheese
60ml/4 tbsp natural (plain) yogurt
90ml/6 tbsp creamy milk
225g/8oz/2 cups cooked white or brown long grain rice
salt and ground black pepper

1 Preheat the oven to 180°C/350°F/Gas 4. Roll out the pastry thinly on a lightly floured surface and use to line a 25cm/10in flan tin (quiche pan). Prick the base all over with a fork and bake for 10–12 minutes, until the pastry is pale golden. (Alternatively, bake blind, having lined the pastry with baking parchment and weighted it with a handful of baking beans.)

2 Heat 30–45ml/2–3 tbsp of the oil in a frying pan. Add the aubergine slices and cook over a medium heat for 6–8 minutes on each side, until golden. You may need to add a little more oil at first, but this will be released as the flesh softens. Remove from the pan with a spatula and drain well on kitchen paper.

3 Add the onion and garlic to the oil remaining in the pan then cook over a gentle heat for 4–5 minutes, until soft, adding a little extra oil if necessary.

4 Rinse the spinach in cold water, drain well and pat dry with kitchen paper. Remove and discard any tough stalks, then chop the spinach leaves finely with a sharp knife or in a food processor. Beat the eggs in a large mixing bowl, then add the spinach, feta, Parmesan, yogurt, milk and the onion mixture. Season to taste with salt and ground black pepper and stir thoroughly to mix.

5 Spread the cooked rice in an even layer over the base of the part-baked pastry case (pie shell). Reserve a few aubergine slices for the top, and arrange the remainder in an even layer over the rice.

6 Spoon the spinach and feta mixture over the aubergines and place the remaining aubergine slices on top. Bake for 30–40 minutes, until lightly browned. Serve the pie while warm, or leave it to cool completely before transferring to a serving plate.

COOK'S TIP

Courgettes (zucchini) could be used in place of the aubergine (eggplant), if you prefer. Cook the sliced courgettes in a little olive oil over a medium heat for 3–4 minutes, until they are evenly golden. You will need to use three or four standard courgettes. Alternatively, choose baby courgettes instead and slice them horizontally.

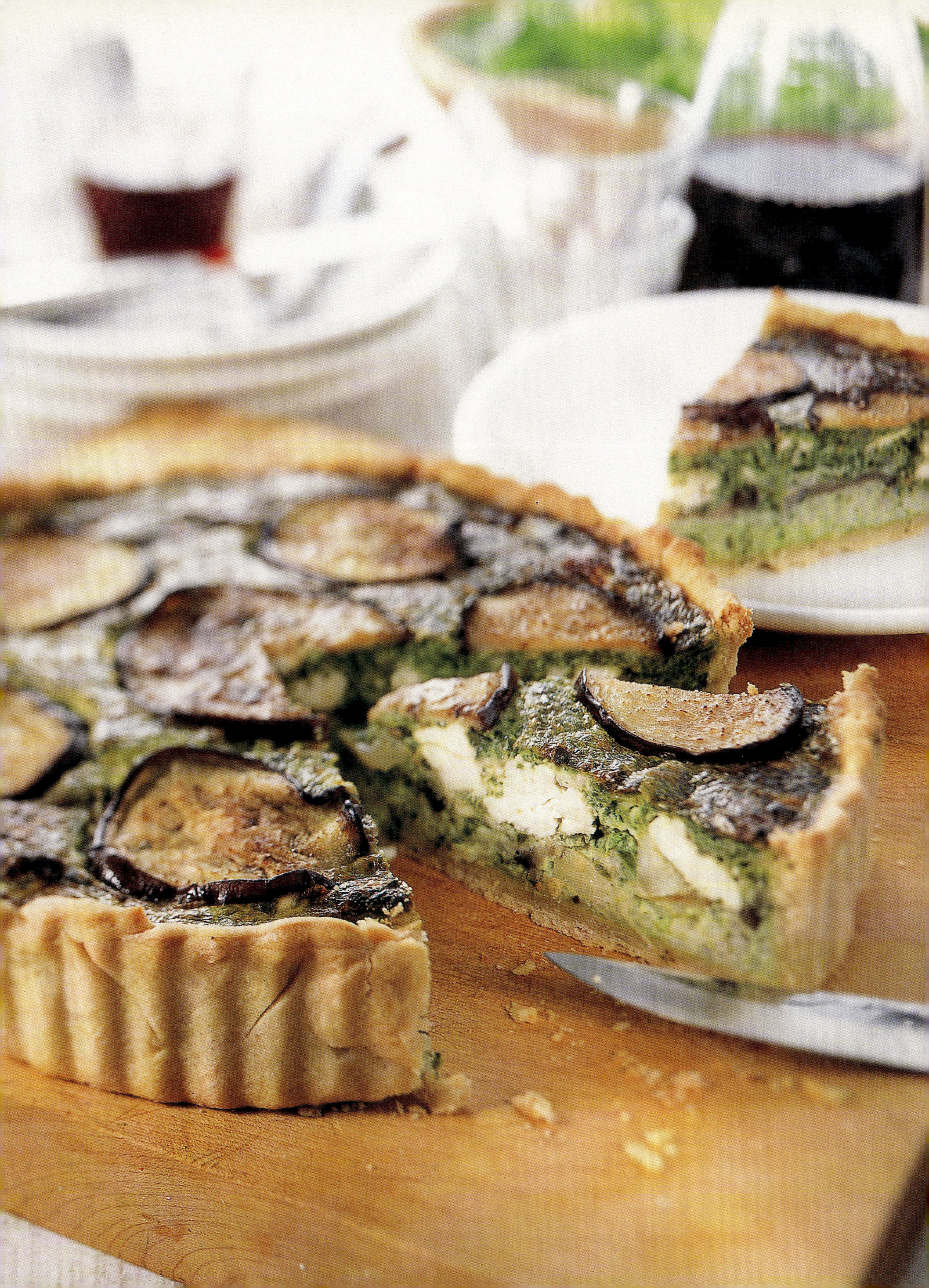

Egg and Salmon Puff Parcels

These crisp elegant parcels hide a mouthwatering collection of flavours and textures, and make a substantial appetizer.

Serves 6

75g/3oz/scant 1/2 cup long grain rice
300ml/1/2 pint/1 1/4 cups fish stock
350g/12oz piece salmon tail
juice of 1/2 lemon
15ml/1 tbsp chopped fresh dill
15ml/1 tbsp chopped fresh parsley
10ml/2 tsp mild curry powder
6 small (US medium) eggs, soft-boiled and cooled
425g/15oz flaky pastry, thawed if frozen
1 small (US medium) egg, beaten
salt and ground black pepper

1 Cook the rice in the fish stock according to the packet instructions, then drain and set aside to cool. Preheat the oven to 220°C/425°F/Gas 7.

2 Poach the salmon in a large pan with just enough water to cover, then remove and discard the bones and skin. Flake the fish into the rice. Add the lemon juice, dill, parsley and curry powder, then season to taste with salt and pepper and mix well. Shell the soft-boiled eggs.

COOK'S TIP
You can also add a spoonful of cooked spinach to each parcel.

3 Roll out the pastry on a floured surface and cut into six 14–15cm/ 5 1/2–6in squares. Brush the edges with the beaten egg. Place a spoonful of the rice mixture in the middle of each square, push an egg into the middle and top with a little more rice.

4 Pull over the pastry corners to the middle to form a square parcel, squeezing the joins together well to seal. Brush with more beaten egg to glaze, place on a baking sheet and bake the puffs for 20 minutes.

5 Reduce the oven temperature to 190°C/375°F/Gas 5 and cook the puffs for a further 10 minutes, or until golden and crisp underneath.

6 Cool slightly before transferring the puffs to serving plates and serving, with a curry flavoured mayonnaise or hollandaise sauce, if you like. Alternatively, serve them on their own.

Thai-style Seafood Turnovers

These elegant appetizer-size turnovers are filled with fish, prawns and fragrant Thai rice.

Makes 18

plain (all-purpose) flour, for dusting
500g/1¼lb puff pastry, thawed if frozen
1 egg, beaten with 30ml/2 tbsp water
lime twists, to garnish

For the filling
275g/10oz skinned white fish fillets
seasoned plain (all-purpose) flour
8–10 large raw prawns (shrimp)
15ml/1 tbsp sunflower oil
about 75g/3oz/6 tbsp butter
6 spring onions (scallions), finely sliced
1 garlic clove, crushed
225g/8oz/2 cups cooked jasmine rice
4cm/1½in piece fresh root ginger, grated
10ml/2 tsp finely chopped fresh coriander (cilantro)
5ml/1 tsp finely grated lime rind

1 Preheat the oven to 190°C/375°F/Gas 5. Make the filling. Cut the fish into 2cm/¾in cubes and dust with seasoned flour, shaking off any excess. Peel and devein the prawns and cut each one into four pieces.

2 Heat half of the oil and 15g/½oz/1 tbsp of the butter in a large frying pan. Add the spring onions and cook gently for 2 minutes.

3 Add the garlic and cook for a further 5 minutes, until the spring onions are very soft. Transfer to a large bowl.

4 Heat the remaining oil and a further 25g/1oz/2 tbsp of the butter in a clean pan. Add the fish pieces and cook briefly. As soon as they begin to turn opaque, use a slotted spoon to transfer them to the bowl with the spring onions.

5 Cook the prawns in the oil mixture remaining in the pan. When they begin to change colour, lift them out with a slotted spoon and add them to the bowl.

6 Add the cooked rice to the bowl, with the fresh root ginger, coriander and grated lime rind. Mix gently, taking care not to break up the fish.

7 Dust the work surface with a little flour. Roll out the pastry and cut into 10cm/4in rounds. Place spoonfuls of filling just off centre on the pastry rounds. Dot with a little of the remaining butter. Dampen the edges of the pastry with a little of the beaten egg mixture, fold one side of the pastry over the filling and press the edges together firmly.

8 Place the turnovers on two lightly greased baking sheets. Decorate them with the pastry trimmings, if you like, and brush them with remaining beaten egg to glaze. Bake the turnovers for 12–15 minutes, or until golden brown all over.

9 Transfer the turnovers to a warm platter and garnish with lime twists, then serve immediately.

Marinated Feta Cheese with Capers

Marinating cubes of feta cheese with herbs and spices gives it a really marvellous flavour.

Serves 6

350g/12oz feta cheese
2 garlic cloves
2.5ml/½ tsp mixed peppercorns
8 coriander seeds
1 bay leaf
15–30ml/1–2 tbsp drained capers
75g/3oz/¾ cup pitted black olives
fresh oregano or thyme sprigs
olive oil, to cover
hot toast and chopped tomatoes, to serve

1 Cut the feta cheese into cubes. Thickly slice the garlic. Put the mixed peppercorns and coriander seeds in a mortar and crush lightly with a pestle.

2 Pack the feta cubes into a large preserving jar with the bay leaf, interspersing layers of cheese with garlic, crushed peppercorns and coriander, capers, olives and the fresh oregano or thyme sprigs.

3 Pour in enough olive oil to cover the cubes of cheese. Close tightly and leave to marinate for 2 weeks in the refrigerator.

4 Lift out the feta cubes and serve on hot toast, with some chopped tomatoes and a little of the flavoured oil from the jar drizzled over.

Cannellini Bean and Rosemary Bruschetta

This sophisticated, Italian variation on the theme of beans on toast makes an unusual party snack.

Serves 6

150g/5oz/⅔ cup dried cannellini beans
5 tomatoes
45ml/3 tbsp olive oil, plus extra for drizzling
2 sun-dried tomatoes in oil, drained and finely chopped
1 garlic clove, crushed
30ml/2 tbsp chopped fresh rosemary
12 slices Italian-style bread, such as ciabatta
1 large garlic clove
salt and ground black pepper
handful of fresh basil leaves, to garnish

1 Put the beans in a bowl, add sufficient cold water to cover and leave to soak overnight.

2 Drain and rinse the beans, then place in a pan and cover with fresh water. Bring to the boil and boil rapidly for 10 minutes. Then simmer for 50–60 minutes, or until tender. Drain, return to the pan and keep warm.

3 Meanwhile, place the tomatoes in a bowl, cover with boiling water; leave for 30 seconds, then peel, seed and chop the flesh. Heat the oil in a frying pan, add the fresh and sun-dried tomatoes, garlic and rosemary. Cook for 2 minutes until the tomatoes begin to break down and soften.

4 Add the tomato mixture to the cannellini beans and season to taste with salt and pepper. Mix together well. Keep the bean mixture warm.

5 Rub the cut sides of the bread slices with the garlic clove, then toast them lightly on both sides. Spoon the cannellini bean mixture evenly on top of the toast. Sprinkle with basil leaves and drizzle with a little extra olive oil before serving.

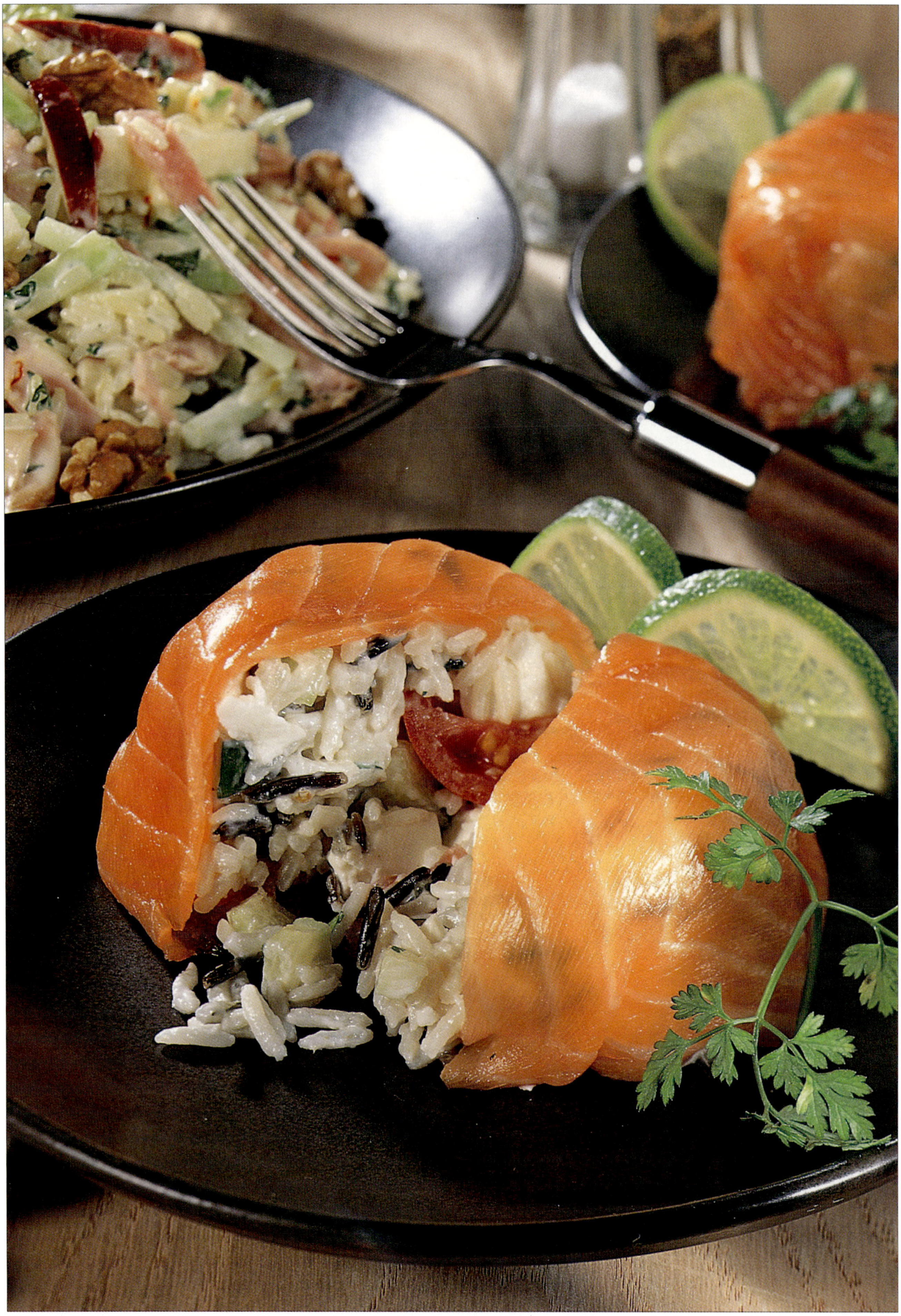

Fish, Meat & Poultry Appetizers

What can match the memorable taste of a properly made Prawn Cocktail? Perhaps Mussels and Clams with Lemon Grass, or a refreshing Melon and Prosciutto Salad. Whatever your preferences there are fish, meat and poultry recipes here to suit all tastes and appetites.

Prawn Cocktail

There is no nicer appetizer than a good, fresh prawn cocktail – and nothing nastier than one in which soggy prawns swim in a thin, vinegary sauce embedded in limp lettuce. This recipe shows just how good a prawn cocktail can be.

Serves 6

60ml/4 tbsp double (heavy) cream, lightly whipped
60ml/4 tbsp mayonnaise, preferably home-made
60ml/4 tbsp tomato ketchup
5–10ml/1–2 tsp Worcestershire sauce
juice of 1 lemon
½ cos or romaine lettuce
450g/1lb/4 cups cooked peeled prawns (shrimp)
salt, ground black pepper and paprika
6 large whole cooked unpeeled prawns (shrimp), to garnish (optional)
thinly sliced brown bread and lemon wedges, to serve

1 Mix together the whipped cream, mayonnaise and ketchup in a bowl. Add Worcestershire sauce to taste. Stir in enough lemon juice to make a really tangy cocktail sauce.

VARIATION
You can also use this mixture for filling vol-au-vents, cold puff pastry cases, to serve as appetizers, canapés or party snacks. The prawns (shrimp) should be chopped before they are mixed with the sauce. Fill the cases just before serving, otherwise they will become soggy and liable to collapse.

2 Finely shred the lettuce and fill six individual glasses one-third full. Gently stir the prawns into the sauce, then taste and adjust the seasoning, if necessary. Spoon the prawn mixture generously over the lettuce.

3 If you like, drape a whole cooked prawn over the edge of each glass (see Cook's Tip). Sprinkle each of the cocktails with ground black pepper and some paprika. Serve the cocktails immediately, with thinly sliced brown bread and butter and lemon wedges for squeezing over.

COOK'S TIP
To prepare the garnish, remove the heads and peel the body shells from the prawns, including the legs, and leave the tail "fan" for decoration.

Marinated Asparagus and Langoustines

For an even more extravagant treat, you could make this attractive salad with medallions of fresh lobster. For a slightly more economical version, use large prawns, allowing six per serving.

Serves 4

16 langoustines
16 fresh asparagus spears, trimmed
2 carrots
30ml/2 tbsp olive oil
1 garlic clove, peeled
salt and ground black pepper
4 fresh tarragon sprigs and some chopped fresh tarragon, to garnish

For the dressing
30ml/2 tbsp tarragon vinegar
120ml/4fl oz/½ cup olive oil

1 Peel the langoustines and keep the discarded parts for making shellfish stock. Set the tail meat aside.

2 Steam the asparagus over a pan of boiling salted water until just tender, but still a little crisp. Refresh under cold water, drain well and place in a shallow dish.

3 Peel the carrots and cut into fine julienne shreds. Cook in a pan of lightly salted, boiling water for about 3 minutes, until tender but still retaining some crunch. Drain, refresh under cold water and drain again. Add to the asparagus.

4 Make the dressing. Whisk the tarragon vinegar with the olive oil in a jug (pitcher). Season to taste with salt and pepper. Pour the dressing over the asparagus and carrots, cover and set aside to marinate.

5 Heat the oil with the garlic in a frying pan until very hot. Add the langoustines and sauté quickly until just heated through. Discard the garlic.

6 Arrange four asparagus spears and a quarter of the carrots on each of four individual plates. Drizzle over the dressing remaining in the dish and top each portion with four langoustine tails. Top with the tarragon sprigs and sprinkle the chopped tarragon on top. Serve immediately.

COOK'S TIP
Langoustines are also known as Dublin Bay prawns, Norway lobster and, when sold already peeled, scampi. Most of the langoustines we buy have been cooked at sea, a necessary act because the flesh deteriorates rapidly after death. Bear this in mind when you cook the shellfish. Because it has already been cooked, it will need to be only lightly sautéed until heated through. If you are lucky enough to buy live langoustines, kill them quickly by immersing them in boiling water, then sauté until cooked through.

Mussels and Clams with Lemon Grass

Lemon grass has an incomparable flavour and is excellent used with a medley of seafood.

Serves 6

1.8–2kg/4–4½ lb fresh mussels
450g/1lb baby clams, washed
120ml/4fl oz/½ cup dry white wine
1 bunch spring onions
    (scallions), chopped
2 lemon grass stalks, chopped
6 kaffir lime leaves, chopped
10ml/2 tsp Thai green curry paste
200ml/7fl oz/scant 1 cup coconut cream
30ml/2 tbsp chopped fresh
    coriander (cilantro)
salt and ground black pepper
whole garlic chives, to garnish

1 Scrub the mussels and pull off the beards. Discard any that are broken or stay open when tapped.

2 Put the wine, spring onions, lemon grass, lime leaves and curry paste in a pan. Simmer over a low heat until the wine has almost evaporated.

COOK'S TIPS
• Buy a few extra mussels just in case there are any which have to be discarded.
• Small, smooth-shelled clams just need rinsing in cold water, but the larger, rough-shelled varieties should be well scrubbed. Like mussels, discard any with broken shells or that are open and do not shut immediately when sharply tapped with a knife.

3 Add the mussels and clams to the pan, cover with a tight-fitting lid and steam the shellfish over a high heat, shaking the pan occasionally, for about 5–6 minutes, until all the shells have opened.

4 Using a slotted spoon, transfer the mussels and clams to a warmed serving bowl and keep hot. Discard any shellfish that remain closed. Strain the cooking liquid through a sieve lined with muslin (cheesecloth) into a clean pan. Set over a low heat and simmer to reduce the quantity to about 250ml/8fl oz/1 cup.

5 Stir in the coconut cream and coriander and season with salt and pepper to taste. Heat through. Pour the sauce over the seafood and serve immediately, garnished with whole garlic chives.

Fish, Meat & Poultry Appetizers **65**

Scallop-stuffed Roast Peppers with Pesto

Serve these scallop-and-pesto-filled sweet red peppers with Italian bread, such as ciabatta or focaccia, to mop up the garlicky juices.

Serves 4

4 squat red (bell) peppers
2 large garlic cloves, cut into thin slivers
60ml/4 tbsp olive oil
4 shelled scallops
45ml/3 tbsp pesto sauce
salt and ground black pepper
freshly grated Parmesan cheese, to serve
salad leaves and basil sprigs, to garnish

1 Preheat the oven to 180°C/350°F/Gas 4. Cut the peppers in half lengthways, through their stalks. Scrape out and discard the cores and seeds. Wash the pepper shells and pat dry with kitchen paper.

2 Put the peppers, cut side up, in an oiled roasting pan. Divide the slivers of garlic equally among them and sprinkle with salt and ground black pepper to taste. Then spoon the olive oil into the peppers and roast for 40 minutes.

3 Using a sharp knife, carefully cut each of the shelled scallops in half horizontally to make two flat discs, each with a piece of coral. When cooked, remove the peppers from the oven and place a scallop half in each pepper half. Then top the scallops with the pesto sauce.

4 Return the roasting pan to the oven and roast for 10 minutes more. Transfer the peppers to individual serving plates, sprinkle with grated Parmesan and garnish each plate with a few salad leaves and basil sprigs. Serve warm.

COOK'S TIP

Scallops are available from most fishmongers and supermarkets with fresh fish counters. Never cook scallops for longer than the time stated in the recipe or they will be tough and rubbery. The orange-coloured corals – scallop roe – are regarded by many as a delicacy, although in the United States and some other countries they are usually discarded.

VARIATION

You could also prepare this dish using red pesto sauce, which is made with sun-dried tomatoes.

Grilled Scallops with Brown Butter

This is a very striking dish as the scallops are served on the half shell, still sizzling from the grill. Reserve it for a special occasion – and special guests.

Serves 4

50g/2oz/¼ cup unsalted (sweet) butter, diced
8 scallops, prepared on the half shell
15ml/1 tbsp chopped fresh parsley
salt and ground black pepper
lemon wedges, to serve

COOK'S TIP
If you can't get hold of scallops in their shells, you can use shelled, fresh scallops if you cook them on the day of purchase. Avoid frozen scallops, as they have a flabby texture.

1 Preheat the grill (broiler) to high. Melt the butter in a small pan over a medium heat. Continue to heat it gently until it is pale golden brown. Remove the pan from the heat immediately – the butter must not be allowed to burn. Arrange the scallops in their half shells in a single layer in a large casserole or a shallow roasting pan. Brush a little of the brown butter over them.

2 Grill (broil) the scallops for 4 minutes – it will not be necessary to turn them. Pour over the remaining brown butter, then season with a little salt and pepper and sprinkle the parsley over them. Serve immediately, with lemon wedges for squeezing over.

Fried Squid

The squid is simply dusted in flour and dipped in egg before being fried, so the coating is light and does not mask the flavour.

Serves 2

115g/4oz prepared squid, cut into rings
30ml/2 tbsp seasoned plain (all-purpose) flour
1 egg
30ml/2 tbsp milk
olive oil, for frying
sea salt, to taste
lemon wedges, to serve

VARIATION
For a crisper coating, dust the rings in flour, then dip them in batter instead of this simple egg and flour coating.

1 Toss the squid rings in the seasoned flour in a bowl or strong plastic bag. Beat the egg and milk together in a shallow bowl. Heat the oil in a large, heavy frying pan.

COOK'S TIP
Keep the squid warm in the oven while you cook the rest.

2 Dip the floured squid rings, one at a time, into the egg mixture, shaking off any excess liquid. Add to the hot oil, in batches if necessary, and cook for 2–3 minutes on each side, until evenly golden all over.

3 Drain the fried squid on kitchen paper, then sprinkle with salt. Transfer to a small warm plate and serve with the lemon wedges.

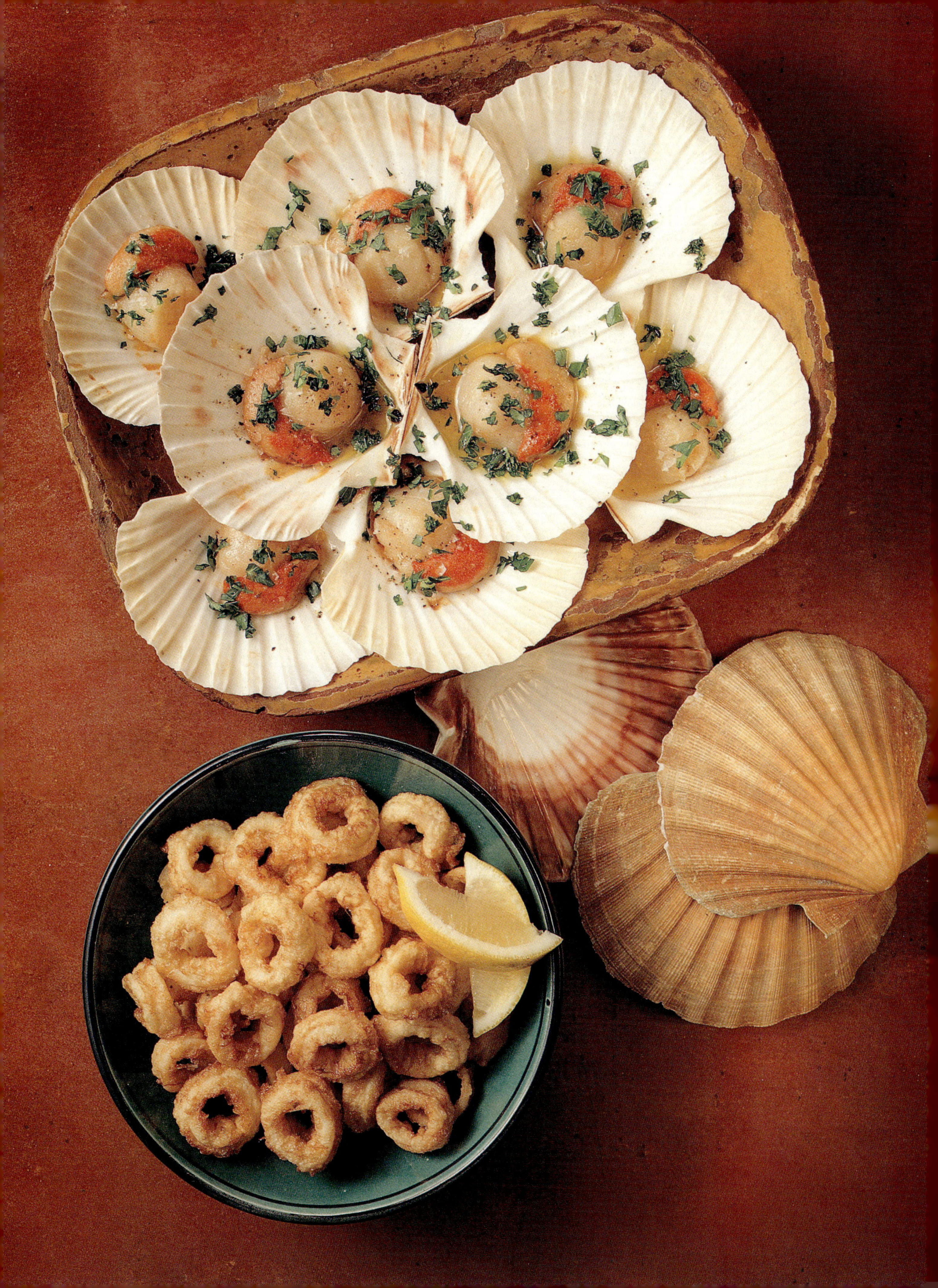

Smoked Salmon and Rice Salad Parcels

Feta, cucumber and tomatoes give a Greek flavour to the salad in these parcels, a combination which goes well with the rice, especially if a little wild rice is added.

Serves 4

175g/6oz/scant 1 cup mixed wild rice and basmati rice
8 slices smoked salmon, total weight about 350g/12oz
10cm/4in piece of cucumber, finely diced
225g/8oz feta cheese, cubed
8 cherry tomatoes, quartered
30ml/2 tbsp mayonnaise
10ml/2 tsp fresh lime juice
15ml/1 tbsp chopped fresh chervil
salt and ground black pepper
lime slices and fresh chervil, to garnish

1 Cook the rice according to the instructions on the packet. Drain, tip into a bowl and leave to cool completely.

2 Line four ramekins with clear film (plastic wrap), then line each ramekin with two slices of smoked salmon, allowing the ends to overlap the edges of the dishes.

VARIATION
You can use other smoked fish in place of the salmon. Smoked trout is an obvious alternative, but you could also try trout, monkfish, freshwater eel or halibut, if you are able to find it.

3 Add the cucumber, cubes of feta and tomato quarters to the rice and stir in the mayonnaise, lime juice and chopped chervil. Mix together well. Season with salt and ground black pepper to taste.

4 Spoon the rice salad mixture into the salmon-lined ramekins. (Any leftover mixture can be used to make a separate rice salad.) Then carefully fold over the overlapping ends of the salmon so that the rice mixture is completely encased.

5 Chill the parcels in the refrigerator for 30–60 minutes, then invert each parcel on to a plate, using the clear film to ease them out of the ramekins. Carefully peel off the clear film, then garnish each parcel with slices of lime and a sprig of fresh chervil and serve.

COOK'S TIP
Wild rice is actually an aquatic grass and is quite expensive, as it is so difficult to harvest. However, a little goes a long way. You can buy packs of mixed wild and long grain rice in most supermarkets.

Deep-fried Whitebait

A spicy coating on these fish gives this favourite dish a crunchy bite.

Serves 6

115g/4oz/1 cup plain (all-purpose) flour
2.5ml/½ tsp curry powder
2.5ml/½ tsp ground ginger
2.5ml/½ tsp cayenne pepper
pinch of salt
1.2kg/2½ lb whitebait, thawed if frozen
vegetable oil, for deep-frying
lemon wedges, to garnish

1 Mix together the plain flour, curry powder, ground ginger, cayenne pepper and a little salt in a large bowl.

2 Coat the fish in the seasoned flour, covering them evenly and shaking off any excess.

3 Heat the oil in a large, heavy pan until it reaches a temperature of 190°C/375°F. Deep-fry the whitebait, in batches, for about 2–3 minutes, until the fish is golden and crisp.

4 Drain the whitebait well on kitchen paper. Keep warm in a low oven until you have cooked all the fish. Serve immediately, garnished with lemon wedges for squeezing over.

Breaded Sole Batons

Goujons of lemon sole are coated in seasoned flour and breadcrumbs, and fried until deliciously crispy.

Serves 4

275g/10oz lemon sole fillets, skinned
2 eggs
115g/4oz/1½ cups fine
  fresh breadcrumbs
75g/3oz/6 tbsp plain (all-purpose) flour
salt and ground black pepper
vegetable oil, for frying
tartare sauce and lemon wedges,
  to serve

1 Cut the fish fillets into long diagonal strips about 2cm/¾in wide, using a sharp knife.

2 Break the eggs into a shallow dish and beat well with a fork. Place the breadcrumbs in another shallow dish. Put the flour in a large plastic bag and season with salt and plenty of ground black pepper.

3 Dip the fish strips into the egg, turning to coat well. Place on a plate and then, taking a few at a time, place them in the bag of flour and shake well to coat. Dip the fish strips in the egg again, then in the breadcrumbs, turning to coat well. Place on a tray in a single layer, not touching. Leave to stand for at least 10 minutes to let the coating set.

4 Heat 1cm/½in oil in a large, heavy frying pan over a medium-high heat. When the oil is hot – a cube of bread will sizzle – add the coated fish strips, in batches, and cook for about 2–2½ minutes, turning once, taking care not to overcrowd the pan. Drain on kitchen paper and keep warm. Serve the fish with tartare sauce and lemon wedges.

Three-colour Fish Kebabs

Don't leave the fish to marinate for more than an hour. The lemon juice will start to break down the fibres of the fish after this time.

Serves 4

120ml/4fl oz/½ cup olive oil
finely grated rind and juice of
   1 large lemon
5ml/1 tsp crushed chilli flakes
350g/12oz monkfish fillet, skinned
   and cubed
350g/12oz swordfish fillet, skinned
   and cubed
350g/12oz thick salmon fillet or
   steak, skinned and cubed
2 red, yellow or orange (bell) peppers,
   seeded and cut into squares
30ml/2 tbsp finely chopped fresh flat
   leaf parsley
salt and ground black pepper

For the sweet tomato and chilli salsa

225g/8oz ripe tomatoes,
   finely chopped
1 garlic clove, crushed
1 fresh red chilli, seeded and chopped
45ml/3 tbsp extra virgin olive oil
15ml/1 tbsp lemon juice
15ml/1 tbsp finely chopped fresh flat
   leaf parsley
pinch of sugar

1 Put the oil in a large, shallow glass or china dish and add the lemon rind and juice, the chilli flakes and pepper to taste. Whisk well to combine, then add all the fish chunks and turn to coat them evenly.

2 Add the pepper squares, stir, then cover with clear film (plastic wrap) and leave to marinate in a cool place for 1 hour, turning the fish occasionally with a slotted spoon.

3 Prepare the barbecue or preheat the grill (broiler) to medium. Thread the chunks of fish and pepper squares on to eight oiled metal skewers, reserving the marinade.

4 Cook the skewers on the barbecue or under the grill, turning once, for 5–8 minutes, until the fish is tender and light golden brown.

5 Meanwhile, make the salsa by mixing the tomatoes, garlic, chilli, olive oil, lemon juice, parsley and sugar in a bowl. Season to taste.

6 Heat the reserved marinade in a small pan to boiling point, then remove the pan from the heat and stir in the parsley and season with salt and pepper to taste.

7 Transfer the kebabs to warm plates, spoon the marinade over them and serve immediately, accompanied by the salsa.

VARIATION
Use tuna instead of swordfish, if you like. It has a similar meaty texture and will be equally successful.

Salade Niçoise

Made with the freshest ingredients, this classic Provençal salad makes a simple yet unbeatable summer dish. Serve with country-style bread and chilled white wine for a Mediterannean treat.

Serves 4–6

115g/4oz green beans
1 tuna steak, about 175g/6oz
olive oil, for brushing
115g/4oz mixed salad leaves
½ small cucumber, thinly sliced
4 ripe tomatoes, quartered
50g/2oz can anchovies, drained and halved lengthways
4 hard-boiled eggs, quartered
½ bunch radishes, trimmed
50g/2oz/½ cup small black olives
salt and ground black pepper
flat leaf parsley, to garnish

For the dressing
90ml/6 tbsp virgin olive oil
2 garlic cloves, crushed
15ml/1 tbsp white wine vinegar
salt and ground black pepper

1 To make the dressing, whisk together the oil, garlic and vinegar in a bowl, then season to taste with salt and pepper.

2 Preheat the grill (broiler). Brush the tuna steak with olive oil and season with salt and black pepper. Grill (broil) for 3–4 minutes on each side, until cooked through. Set aside to cool.

3 Trim and halve the green beans. Cook them in a pan of boiling water for 2 minutes, until only just tender, then drain, refresh under cold water and leave to cool.

4 Mix together the salad leaves, sliced cucumber, tomatoes and green beans in a large, shallow bowl. Flake the cooled tuna steak with your fingers or two forks.

5 Sprinkle the tuna, anchovies, eggs, radishes and olives over the salad. Pour over the dressing and toss together lightly. Serve garnished with parsley.

COOK'S TIP

For an authentic touch, use black Nice olives and Nice mesclun – a mixture of frisée lettuce, lamb's lettuce, dandelion, rocket (arugula), chervil, purslane, young spinach leaves and oak leaf lettuce.

Caesar Salad

This is a well-known and much enjoyed salad invented by a chef called Caesar Cardini. Be sure to use crisp lettuce and add the very soft eggs at the last minute.

Serves 6

175ml/6fl oz/¾ cup salad oil, preferably olive oil
115g/4oz French or Italian bread, cut in 2.5cm/1in cubes
1 large garlic clove, crushed with the flat side of a knife
1 cos or romaine lettuce
2 eggs, boiled for 1 minute
120ml/4fl oz/½ cup lemon juice
50g/2oz/⅔ cup freshly grated Parmesan cheese
6 canned anchovy fillets, drained and finely chopped (optional)
salt and ground black pepper

1 Heat 50ml/2fl oz/¼ cup of the oil in a large frying pan. Add the bread cubes and garlic. Cook over a medium heat, stirring and turning constantly, until the bread cubes are golden brown all over. Drain well on kitchen paper. Discard the garlic.

2 Tear large lettuce leaves into smaller pieces. Put all the lettuce in a bowl.

COOK'S TIP
Do not boil the eggs for longer than 1 minute. The whites should be milky, while the yolks remain raw.

3 Add the remaining oil to the lettuce and season with salt and plenty of ground black pepper. Toss well to coat the leaves.

4 Break the eggs on top. Sprinkle with the lemon juice. Toss thoroughly again to combine.

5 Add the Parmesan cheese and anchovies, if using. Toss gently to mix.

6 Sprinkle the fried bread cubes on top and serve immediately.

VARIATIONS
• To make a tangier dressing mix 30ml/ 2 tbsp white wine vinegar, 15ml/1 tbsp Worcestershire sauce, 2.5ml/½ tsp mustard powder, 5ml/1 tsp sugar, salt and pepper in a screw-top jar, then add the oil and shake well.
• If you are worried about the safety of eating very lightly cooked eggs, you can substitute quartered hard-boiled eggs. However, the dressing will not be as creamy without the runny egg yolk.

Avocado and Smoked Fish Salad

Avocado and smoked fish make a good combination, and flavoured with herbs and spices, create a delectable and elegant salad.

Serves 4

15g/½oz/1 tbsp butter
  or margarine
½ onion, thinly sliced
5ml/1 tsp mustard seeds
225g/8oz smoked mackerel, flaked
30ml/2 tbsp chopped fresh
  coriander (cilantro)
2 firm tomatoes, peeled
  and chopped
15ml/1 tbsp lemon juice

For the salad

2 avocados, halved, stoned (pitted)
  and peeled
½ cucumber
15ml/1 tbsp lemon juice
2 firm tomatoes
1 green chilli
salt and ground black pepper

1 Melt the butter or margarine in a heavy frying pan, add the onion and mustard seeds and cook over a low heat, stirring occasionally, for about 5 minutes, until the onion is soft but not browned.

2 Add the flaked mackerel, chopped coriander, tomatoes and lemon juice and cook over a low heat for about 2–3 minutes. Remove the pan from the heat and leave to cool.

COOK'S TIP
Although smoked mackerel has a very distinctive flavour, smoked haddock or cod can also be used in this salad, or a mixture of mackerel and haddock. For a speedy salad when time is short, canned tuna makes an easy and convenient substitute.

3 To make the salad, thinly slice the avocados and cucumber. Place them together in a bowl and sprinkle with the lemon juice to prevent the avocado flesh from discolouring.

4 Slice the tomatoes and seed and finely chop the chilli.

5 Place the fish mixture in the centre of a serving plate.

6 Arrange the avocado slices, cucumber and tomatoes decoratively around the outside of the fish mixture. Alternatively, spoon a quarter of the fish mixture on to each of four individual serving plates and divide the avocados, cucumber and tomatoes equally among them. Then sprinkle with the chopped chilli, season with a little salt and ground black pepper and serve immediately.

Stuffed Garlic Mushrooms with Prosciutto

Field mushrooms can vary greatly in size. Try to find similar-sized specimens with undamaged edges.

Serves 4

8 field (portabello) mushrooms
15g/½oz/¼ cup dried ceps, bay boletus or saffron milk-caps, soaked in warm water for 20 minutes
75g/3oz/6 tbsp unsalted (sweet) butter
1 onion, chopped
1 garlic clove, crushed
75g/3oz/¾ cup fresh breadcrumbs
1 egg
75ml/5 tbsp chopped fresh parsley
15ml/1 tbsp chopped fresh thyme
salt and ground black pepper
115g/4oz prosciutto di Parma or San Daniele, thinly sliced
fresh parsley, to garnish

1 Preheat the oven to 190°C/375°F/Gas 5. Carefully break off the stems of the field mushrooms, without damaging the caps. Set the caps aside. Finely chop the stems. Drain the dried mushrooms and chop finely.

2 Melt half the butter in a large, heavy frying pan until foaming. Add the onion and cook over a low heat, stirring occasionally, for 6–8 minutes, until softened but not coloured.

3 Add the garlic, dried mushroom and chopped mushroom stems to the pan and cook, stirring occasionally, for about 2–3 minutes.

4 Transfer the mixture to a bowl, add the breadcrumbs, egg, parsley and thyme and season to taste with salt and pepper. Melt the remaining butter in a small pan and generously brush over the reserved mushroom caps. Arrange the mushroom caps on a baking sheet and spoon in the filling. Bake for 20–25 minutes, until they are well browned and tender.

5 Top each mushroom with a slice of prosciutto, garnish with parsley and serve immediately.

COOK'S TIPS
- Garlic mushrooms can be easily prepared in advance ready to go into the oven when your guests arrive.
- Fresh breadcrumbs can be made and then frozen. They can be taken from the freezer as they are required and do not need to be thawed first.
- Prosciutto is a dry-cured ham and opinions on whether Parma or San Daniele ham is superior differ. You could also use Jambon de Bayonne, Lomo Ahumado or Smithfield ham.

Melon and Prosciutto Salad

Sections of cool fragrant melon wrapped with slices of air-dried ham make a delicious salad appetizer. If strawberries are in season, serve with a savoury-sweet strawberry salsa and watch it disappear.

Serves 4

1 large cantaloupe, Charentais or Galia melon
175g/6oz prosciutto or Serrano ham, thinly sliced

For the salsa
225g/8oz/2 cups strawberries
5ml/1 tsp caster (superfine) sugar
30ml/2 tbsp sunflower oil
15ml/1 tbsp orange juice
2.5ml/½ tsp finely grated orange rind
2.5ml/½ tsp finely grated fresh root ginger
salt and ground black pepper

1 Halve the melon, scoop out the seeds with a spoon and discard. Cut the rind away with a paring knife, then slice the melon thickly. Chill in the refrigerator until ready to serve.

2 For the salsa, hull the strawberries and cut them into large dice. Place in a small mixing bowl with the sugar and crush very lightly to release the juices. Add the sunflower oil, orange juice, orange rind and grated ginger. Season with a little salt and plenty of ground black pepper.

3 Arrange the melon slices on a serving plate, lay the prosciutto or Serrano ham over the top and then serve with a bowl of salsa, handed around separately.

Mushroom Salad with Prosciutto

Pancake ribbons give a lovely light texture to this salad. Use whatever edible wild mushrooms you can find, or substitute interesting cultivated varieties if you need to.

Serves 4

40g/1½ oz/3 tbsp unsalted (sweet) butter
450g/1lb assorted wild and cultivated mushrooms such as chanterelles, ceps, bay boletus, oyster, field (portabello) and Paris mushrooms, trimmed and sliced
60ml/4 tbsp Madeira or sherry
juice of ½ lemon
½ oak leaf lettuce
½ frisée lettuce
30ml/2 tbsp walnut oil
salt and ground black pepper

For the pancake and ham ribbons
25g/1oz/3 tbsp plain (all-purpose) flour
75ml/5 tbsp milk
1 egg
60ml/4 tbsp freshly grated Parmesan cheese
60ml/4 tbsp chopped fresh herbs such as parsley, thyme, marjoram or chives
salt and ground black pepper
butter, for frying
175g/6oz prosciutto, thickly sliced

1 To make the pancakes, blend the flour and the milk. Beat in the egg, cheese, herbs and some seasoning. Heat the butter in a frying pan and pour enough of the mixture to coat the base. When the batter has set, turn the pancake over and cook until firm.

2 Turn out and cool. Roll up the pancake and slice to make 1cm/½in ribbons. Cook the remaining batter the same way and cut the ham into similar sized ribbons. Toss with the pancake ribbons. Set aside.

3 Gently fry the mushrooms in the butter for 6–8 minutes, until the moisture has evaporated. Add the Madeira or sherry and lemon juice and season to taste.

4 Toss the salad leaves in the oil and arrange on four plates. Place the prosciutto and pancake ribbons in the centre, spoon on the mushrooms and serve immediately.

Yakitori Chicken

These Japanese-style kebabs are easy to eat and ideal for barbecues or parties.

Makes 12

6 boneless, skinless chicken thighs
1 bunch of spring onions (scallions)
shichimi (seven-flavour spice),
 to serve (optional)

For the yakitori sauce
150ml/¼ pint/⅔ cup Japanese
 soy sauce
90g/3½oz/½ cup sugar
25ml/1½ tbsp sake or dry white wine
15ml/1 tbsp plain (all-purpose) flour

1 Soak 12 wooden skewers in water for at least 30 minutes. Make the sauce. Stir the soy sauce, sugar and sake or wine into the flour in a small pan and bring to the boil, stirring. Lower the heat and simmer the mixture for 10 minutes, or until the sauce is reduced by one-third. Set aside.

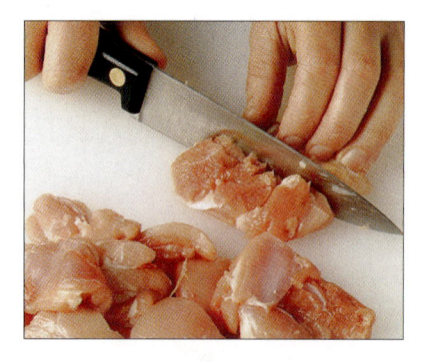

2 Cut each chicken thigh into bitesize pieces and set aside.

3 Cut the spring onions into 3cm/1¼ in pieces. Preheat the grill (broiler) or prepare the barbecue.

COOK'S TIP
If shichimi is difficult to obtain, paprika can be used instead.

4 Thread the chicken and spring onions alternately on to the drained skewers. Grill (broil) under a medium heat or cook on the barbecue, brushing generously several times with the sauce. Allow 5–10 minutes, or until the chicken is cooked but still moist.

5 Serve with yakitori sauce, offering shichimi with the kebabs if available.

VARIATION
Bitesize chunks of turkey breast fillet, lean boneless pork or lamb fillet can be used instead of chicken. Small, whole button (white) mushrooms are also delicious for a vegetarian alternative.

Chicken Bitki

This is a popular Polish dish and makes an attractive appetizer when offset by deep red beetroot.

Makes 12

15g/½oz/1 tbsp butter, melted
115g/4oz flat mushrooms, finely chopped
50g/2oz/1 cup fresh white breadcrumbs
350g/12oz skinless chicken breast portions or guinea fowl, minced (ground) or finely chopped
2 eggs, separated
1.5ml/¼ tsp grated nutmeg
30ml/2 tbsp plain (all-purpose) flour
45ml/3 tbsp vegetable oil
salt and ground black pepper
salad leaves and grated pickled beetroot (beet), to serve

1 Melt the butter in a pan and cook the mushrooms for about 5 minutes, until softened and the juices have evaporated. Leave to cool.

2 Mix together the mushrooms, breadcrumbs, minced or chopped chicken or guinea fowl, egg yolks and nutmeg in a bowl and season to taste with salt and pepper.

3 Whisk the egg whites until stiff in a clean, grease-free bowl. Gently stir half the whites into the chicken or guinea fowl mixture to slacken it, then fold in the remainder with a rubber spatula or metal spoon.

4 Shape the mixture into 12 even-size meatballs, about 7.5cm/3in long and 2.5cm/1in wide. Spread out the flour on a shallow plate. Roll the meatballs in the flour to coat.

5 Heat the oil in a large, heavy frying pan, add the bitki and cook over a medium heat for about 10 minutes, turning occasionally until evenly golden brown and cooked through. Serve hot with salad leaves and grated pickled beetroot.

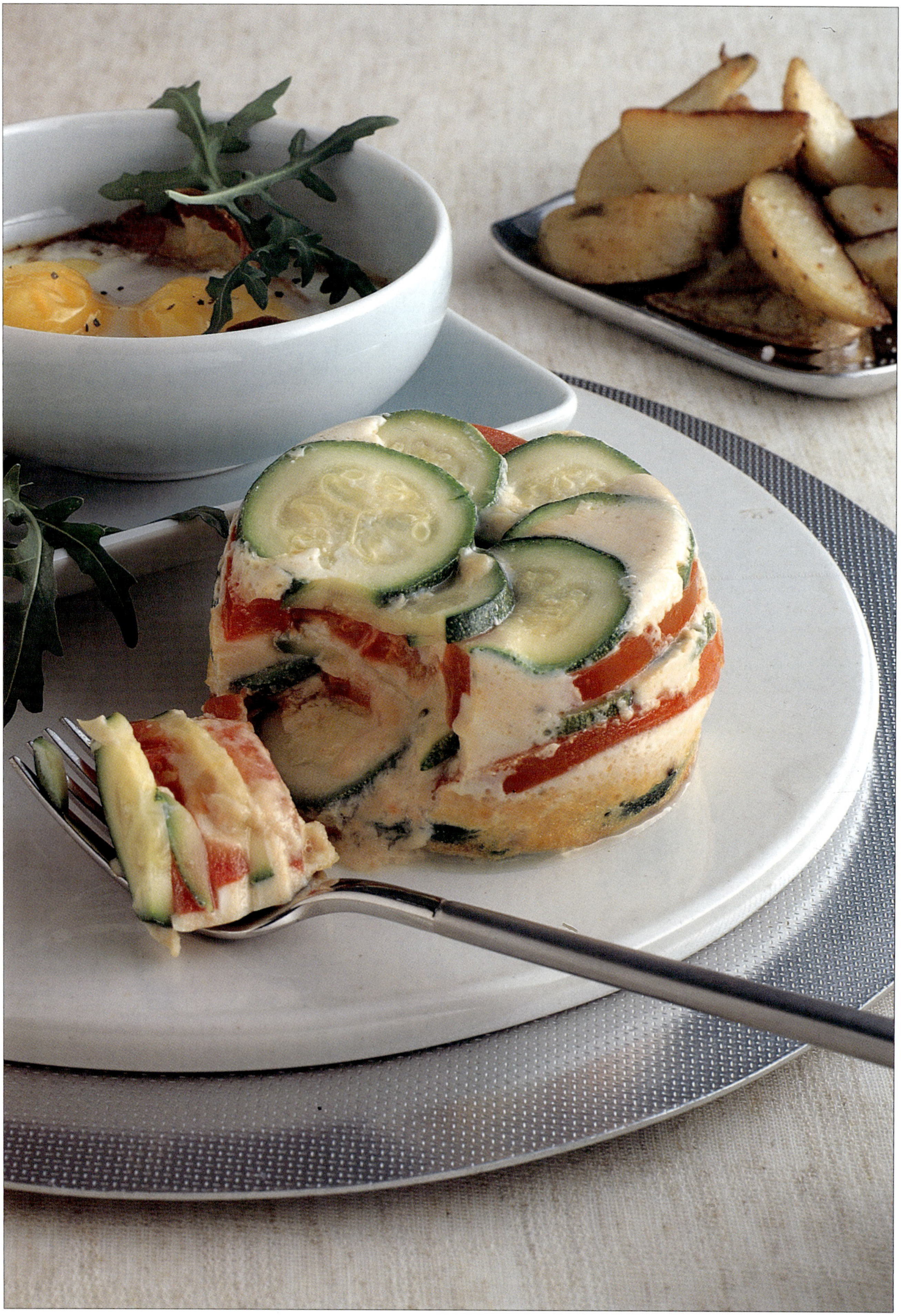

Vegetarian Dishes

The freshest of vegetables cooked with the lightest of touches can be unforgettable. Tomato and Courgette Timbales are undeniably elegant, a classic Risotto alla Milanese is perfect for a winter's day and there's nothing like a simple Tricolor Salad for al fresco dining.

Pears and Stilton

This is a traditional English dish and a marriage made in heaven. The flavours and textures of pears and cheese are simply superb together.

Serves 4

4 ripe pears, lightly chilled
75g/3oz blue Stilton
50g/2oz curd (farmer's) cheese
ground black pepper
watercress sprigs, to garnish

For the dressing
45ml/3 tbsp light olive oil
15ml/1 tbsp lemon juice
10ml/2 tsp toasted poppy seeds
salt and ground black pepper

1 First make the dressing. Place the olive oil and lemon juice, poppy seeds and seasoning to taste in a screw-top jar and then shake together vigorously until emulsified.

COOK'S TIPS
• Comice pears are a good choice for this dish, being very juicy and aromatic. For a dramatic colour contrast, select the excellent sweet and juicy Red Williams or Red Bartletts.
• You can mix the cheese filling in advance and store, covered with clear film (plastic wrap) in the refrigerator. Similarly, mix the dressing ahead of time, but bring it to room temperature to serve. However, don't halve the pears until just before serving or the flesh will discolour, becoming an unappetizing brown.

2 Cut the pears in half lengthways, then scoop out the cores and cut away the calyx from the rounded end.

3 Place the Stilton and curd cheese in a bowl and beat together, then season with a little pepper and beat lightly again. Divide this mixture among the cavities in the pears.

4 Shake the dressing to mix it again, then spoon it over the pears. Serve garnished with some watercress sprigs.

VARIATION
Stilton is the classic British blue cheese, but you could use Blue Cheshire or even a non-British cheese, such as Gorgonzola or Roquefort, if you like.

Goat's Cheese Salad

Goat's cheese has a strong, tangy flavour, so choose robust salad leaves to accompany it.

Serves 4

30ml/2 tbsp olive oil
4 slices of French bread, 1cm/½ in thick
8 cups mixed salad leaves, such as frisée lettuce, radicchio and red oak leaf, torn in small pieces
4 firm goat's cheese rounds, about 50g/2oz each, rind removed
1 yellow or red (bell) pepper, seeded and finely diced
1 small red onion, thinly sliced
45ml/3 tbsp chopped fresh parsley
30ml/2 tbsp chopped fresh chives

For the dressing
30ml/2 tbsp white wine vinegar
1.5ml/¼ tsp salt
5ml/1 tsp wholegrain mustard
75ml/5 tbsp olive oil
ground black pepper

1 To make the dressing, mix the vinegar and salt in a bowl or jug (pitcher), stirring with a fork until the salt has dissolved. Stir in the mustard. Gradually whisk in the olive oil until blended. Season to taste with pepper and set aside until needed.

2 Preheat the grill (broiler). Heat the oil in a frying pan. Add the bread slices and cook for about 1 minute, until the undersides are golden. Turn and cook on the other side for about 30 seconds more. Drain well on kitchen paper and set aside.

3 Place the salad leaves in a bowl. Add 45ml/3 tbsp of the dressing and toss to coat well. Divide the dressed leaves among four salad plates.

4 Place the goat's cheeses on a baking sheet and grill (broil) for about 1–2 minutes, until bubbling and golden.

COOK'S TIP
Cheese made entirely from goat's milk is usually labelled "pure" or, if French, "chèvre". Milder cheeses are made with a mixture of cow's and goat's milk.

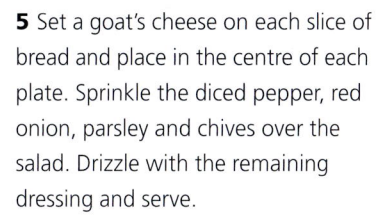

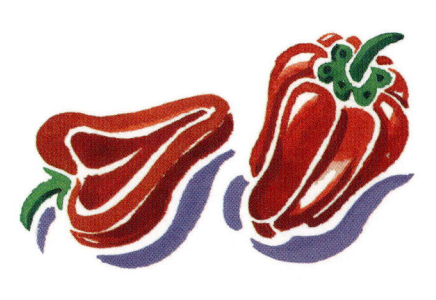

5 Set a goat's cheese on each slice of bread and place in the centre of each plate. Sprinkle the diced pepper, red onion, parsley and chives over the salad. Drizzle with the remaining dressing and serve.

Asparagus and Orange Salad

A simple dressing of olive oil and sherry vinegar mingles with the orange and tomato flavours with great results.

Serves 4

225g/8oz asparagus, trimmed and cut into 5cm/2in pieces
2 large oranges
2 well-flavoured ripe tomatoes, cut into eighths
50g/2oz romaine lettuce leaves, shredded
30ml/2 tbsp extra virgin olive oil
2.5ml/½ tsp sherry vinegar
salt and ground black pepper

1 Cook the asparagus in lightly salted, boiling water for 3–4 minutes, until just tender. Drain and refresh under cold water. Set aside.

2 Grate the rind from half an orange and reserve. Peel both oranges and cut into segments, leaving the membrane behind. Squeeze out the juice from the membrane and reserve the juice.

COOK'S TIP
Sherry vinegar is golden brown with a rounded and full flavour. It is matured in wooden barrels in much the same way as sherry itself.

3 Put the asparagus pieces, segments of orange, tomatoes and lettuce into a salad bowl. Mix together the olive oil and sherry vinegar and add 15ml/1 tbsp of the reserved orange juice and 5ml/1 tsp of the grated orange rind, whisking well to combine. Season with a little salt and plenty of ground black pepper. Just before serving, pour the dressing over the salad and mix gently to coat.

Tricolor Salad

A popular salad, this dish depends for its success on the quality of its ingredients. Mozzarella di bufala is the best cheese to serve uncooked. Whole ripe plum tomatoes give up their juice to blend with extra virgin olive oil for a natural dressing.

Serves 4

300g/11oz mozzarella di bufala cheese, thinly sliced
8 large plum tomatoes, sliced
1 large avocado
about 15 basil leaves or a small handful of flat leaf parsley leaves
90–120ml/6–8 tbsp extra virgin olive oil
ground black pepper
ciabatta and sea salt flakes, to serve

1 Arrange the mozzarella cheese slices and tomato slices randomly on four salad plates. Crush over a few good pinches of sea salt flakes. This will help to draw out some of the juices from the plum tomatoes. Cover with clear film (plastic wrap), set aside in a cool place and leave to marinate for about 30 minutes.

2 Just before serving, cut the avocado in half lengthways, using a large, sharp knife and twist the halves to separate them. Lift out the stone (pit) with the point of the knife and remove the peel.

3 Carefully slice the avocado flesh crossways into half moons, or cut it into large chunks if that is easier.

4 Place the avocado slices on the salad, then sprinkle with the basil or parsley. Drizzle over the olive oil, add a little more salt if you like and season well with black pepper. Serve the salad at room temperature, with chunks of crusty Italian ciabatta or other country bread for mopping up the dressing.

Panzanella Salad

If sliced, juicy tomatoes layered with day-old bread sounds strange for a salad, don't be deceived – it's quite delicious. A popular Italian salad, this dish is ideal for entertaining.

Serves 4–6

4 thick slices day-old bread, either white, brown or rye
1 small red onion
450g/1lb ripe tomatoes, thinly sliced
115g/4oz mozzarella cheese, thinly sliced
5ml/1 tbsp fresh basil, shredded, or fresh marjoram
120ml/4fl oz/½ cup extra virgin olive oil
45ml/3 tbsp balsamic vinegar
juice or 1 small lemon
salt and ground black pepper
pitted and sliced black olives or salted capers, to garnish

1 Dip the bread briefly in a shallow dish of cold water, then carefully squeeze out the excess water. Arrange the bread in the base of a shallow salad bowl.

2 Thinly slice the onion, then soak the slices in a separate bowl of cold water for about 10 minutes while you prepare the other ingredients. This helps to reduce the astringency of the onion, so that it does not overpower the other flavours. Drain and reserve.

3 Layer the tomatoes, cheese, onion, basil or marjoram in the salad bowl, seasoning well with salt and pepper in between each layer. Sprinkle the salad with the olive oil, balsamic vinegar and lemon juice.

4 Top with the olives or capers. Cover with clear film (plastic wrap) and chill the salad in the refrigerator for at least 2 hours, or overnight, if possible.

Courgette Fritters with Chilli Jam

Chilli jam is hot, sweet and sticky – rather like a thick chutney. It adds a delicious piquancy to these light courgette fritters which are always a popular dish.

Makes 12 fritters

450g/1lb/3½ cups coarsely grated
   courgettes (zucchini)
50g/2oz/⅔ cup freshly grated
   Parmesan cheese
2 eggs, beaten
60ml/4 tbsp plain (all-purpose) flour
vegetable oil, for frying
salt and ground black pepper

For the chilli jam
75ml/5 tbsp olive oil
4 large onions, diced
4 garlic cloves, chopped
1–2 green chillies, seeded and sliced
30ml/2 tbsp dark brown soft sugar

1 First make the chilli jam. Heat the oil in a large, heavy frying pan, then add the onions and the garlic. Reduce the heat to low, then cook for 20 minutes, stirring frequently, until the onions are very soft.

VARIATION
If you don't like chillies or you are short of time, serve the fritters with an easy-to-make dip. Chop a bunch of spring onions (scallions) and stir them into a 150ml/5fl oz/⅔ cup sour cream or simply mix finely chopped fresh herbs into a bowl of good-quality mayonnaise.

2 Remove the pan from the heat and leave the onion mixture to cool, then transfer to a food processor or blender. Add the chillies and sugar and process until smooth, then return the mixture to the pan. Cook over a low heat for a further 10 minutes, stirring frequently, until the liquid evaporates and the mixture has the consistency of jam. Cool slightly.

3 To make the fritters, squeeze the courgettes in a dishtowel to remove any excess liquid, then combine with the grated Parmesan, eggs and flour and season with salt and pepper.

COOK'S TIP
Stored in an airtight jar in the refrigerator, the chilli jam will keep for up to 1 week.

4 Pour in enough oil to cover the base of a large frying pan and heat. Add 30ml/2 tbsp of the courgette mixture for each fritter and cook three fritters at a time. Cook for 2–3 minutes on each side until golden, then keep warm while you cook the rest of the fritters. Drain well on kitchen paper and serve warm with a spoonful of the chilli jam.

Aubergine and Smoked Mozzarella Rolls

Slices of grilled aubergine are stuffed with smoked mozzarella, tomato and fresh basil to make an attractive hors-d'oeuvre.

Serves 4

1 large aubergine (eggplant)
45ml/3 tbsp olive oil, plus extra for drizzling (optional)
165g/5½ oz smoked mozzarella cheese, cut into 8 slices
2 plum tomatoes, each cut into 4 even-size slices
8 large basil leaves
balsamic vinegar, for drizzling (optional)
salt and ground black pepper

1 Cut the aubergine lengthways into 10 thin slices and discard the two outermost slices. Sprinkle the slices with salt and set them aside for 20 minutes. Rinse well under cold running water to remove all traces of salt, then drain and pat dry with kitchen paper.

2 Prepare the barbecue or preheat the grill (broiler) and line the rack with foil. Place the aubergine slices on the rack and brush liberally with oil. Cook for 8–10 minutes until tender and golden, turning once.

3 Remove the aubergine slices from the heat, then place a slice of mozzarella, a slice of tomato and a basil leaf in the centre of each aubergine slice, and season to taste. Fold the aubergine over the filling and return to the heat, seam side down, until heated through and the mozzarella begins to melt. Serve drizzled with olive oil and a little balsamic vinegar, if using.

Fried Rice Balls Stuffed with Mozzarella

These deep-fried balls of risotto go by the name of *Suppli al Telefono* in their native Italy because the strings of melted mozzarella resemble telephone wires. Stuffed with mozzarella cheese, they are very popular snacks, which is hardly surprising as they are quite delicious. They make wonderful party bites or a great start to any dinner party meal.

Serves 8

1 quantity Risotto alla Milanese
3 eggs
breadcrumbs and plain (all-purpose) flour, for dusting
115g/4oz mozzarella cheese, cut into small cubes
vegetable oil, for deep-frying
dressed frisée lettuce leaves and cherry tomatoes, to serve (optional)

1 Put the risotto in a bowl and leave it to cool completely. Beat two of the eggs and stir them into the cooled risotto until well mixed.

2 Use your hands to form the rice mixture into balls the size of a large egg. If the mixture is too moist to hold its shape well, stir in a few spoonfuls of breadcrumbs.

3 Poke a hole in the centre of each ball with your finger, then fill it with small cubes of mozzarella and close the hole over again with the rice mixture.

COOK'S TIP
These provide the perfect solution for the problem of to what to do with leftover risotto, as they are best made with a cold mixture, cooked the day before. This also makes them a perfect choice for parties as much of the preparation is done ahead.

4 Heat the oil for deep-frying until a small piece of bread sizzles as soon as it is dropped in.

5 Spread out some flour on a plate. Beat the remaining egg in a shallow bowl. Sprinkle another plate with breadcrumbs. Roll the risotto balls in the flour, then in the egg and, finally, in the breadcrumbs.

6 Deep-fry the rice balls, a few at a time, in the hot oil until golden and crisp. Drain on kitchen paper while the remaining balls are being fried, and keep warm. Transfer to warm plates and serve immediately, with dressed frisée leaves and cherry tomatoes if serving as an appetizer. For finger food, transfer to a warm platter and serve plain.

Tomato and Courgette Timbales

Timbales are baked savoury custards typical of the south of France, and mainly made with light vegetables. This combination is delicious as an appetizer. It can be served warm or cool.

Serves 4

butter, for greasing
2 courgettes (zucchini), about 175g/6oz
2 firm, ripe vine tomatoes, sliced
2 eggs plus 2 egg yolks
45ml/3 tbsp double (heavy) cream
15ml/1 tbsp fresh tomato sauce or passata (bottled strained tomatoes)
10ml/2 tsp chopped fresh basil or oregano or 5ml/1 tsp dried oregano
salt and ground black pepper
salad leaves, to serve

1 Preheat the oven to 180°C/350°F/Gas 4. Lightly butter four large ramekins. Trim the courgettes, then cut them into thin slices. Put them into a steamer and steam over boiling water for 4–5 minutes.

2 Drain the courgette slices well in a colander, then layer them in the prepared ramekins alternating with the sliced tomatoes.

3 Whisk together the eggs, cream, tomato sauce or passata and basil or oregano in a bowl. Season to taste with salt and pepper.

4 Pour the egg mixture into the ramekins. Place them in a roasting pan and half fill the pan with hot water. Bake the ramekins for 20–30 minutes, until the custard is just firm.

5 Cool slightly, then run a knife blade around the rims of the ramekins and carefully turn out on to small plates. Serve with salad leaves.

COOK'S TIP
Don't overcook the timbales or the texture of the savoury custard will become rubbery.

Poached Eggs Florentine

The term "à la Florentine" means "in the style of Florence", referring to dishes cooked with spinach and topped with mornay sauce.

Serves 4

675g/1½lb spinach
25g/1oz/2 tbsp butter
60ml/4 tbsp double (heavy) cream
pinch of freshly grated nutmeg
salt and ground black pepper

For the topping

25g/1oz/2 tbsp butter
25g/1oz/¼ cup plain
　(all-purpose) flour
300ml/½ pint/1¼ cups hot milk
pinch of ground mace
115g/4oz/1 cup grated Gruyère cheese
4 eggs
15ml/1 tbsp grated Parmesan cheese,
　plus shavings to serve

1 Cut off any tough stalks, then wash the spinach in cold water and drain well. Place it in a large pan with very little water. Cook over a medium heat for 3–4 minutes, or until tender and wilted, then drain thoroughly and chop finely. Return the spinach to the pan, add the butter, cream and grated nutmeg and season to taste with salt and pepper, then heat through gently, stirring occasionally. Spoon the spinach mixture into the base of one large or four small gratin dishes.

2 To make the topping, heat the butter in a small pan, add the flour and cook, stirring constantly, for 1 minute to make a paste. Gradually blend in the hot milk, beating well as it thickens to break up any lumps.

3 Cook for 1–2 minutes, stirring constantly. Remove the pan from the heat and stir in the mace and three-quarters of the Gruyère.

4 Preheat the oven to 200°C/400°F/Gas 6. Poach the eggs, one at a time, in lightly salted water for 3–4 minutes. Make hollows in the spinach with the back of a spoon, and place a poached egg in each one. Cover with the cheese sauce and sprinkle with the remaining Gruyère and the grated Parmesan. Bake for 10 minutes, or until golden. Serve immediately with Parmesan shavings.

Risotto alla Milanese

This classic risotto is often served with the hearty veal stew, osso bucco. Serve a larger portion for a delicious light meal..

Serves 8

about 1.2 litres/2 pints/5 cups vegetable stock
good pinch of saffron threads
75g/3oz/6 tbsp butter
1 onion, finely chopped
275g/10oz/1½ cups risotto rice
75g/3oz/1 cup freshly grated Parmesan cheese
salt and ground black pepper

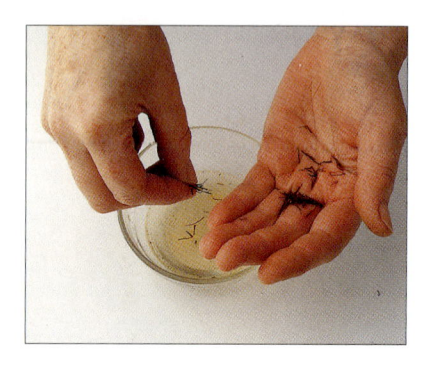

1 Bring the stock to the boil in a large pan, then reduce to a low simmer. Ladle a little hot stock into a small bowl. Add the saffron threads and set aside to infuse (steep).

2 Melt 50g/2oz/4 tbsp of the butter in a large, heavy pan until foaming. Add the onion and cook over a low heat, stirring occasionally, for about 3 minutes, until softened and translucent but not browned.

3 Add the rice. Stir until the grains are coated with butter and starting to swell and burst, then add a few ladlefuls of the hot stock, with the saffron liquid and salt and pepper to taste. Stir constantly over a low heat until all the stock has been absorbed. Add the remaining stock, a few ladlefuls at a time, allowing the rice to absorb all the liquid before adding more, and stirring constantly. After about 20–25 minutes, the rice should be just tender and the risotto golden yellow, moist and creamy.

4 Gently stir in about two-thirds of the grated Parmesan and the remaining butter. Heat through gently until the butter has melted, then taste and adjust the seasoning, if necessary. Transfer the risotto to a warmed serving bowl or platter and serve hot, with the remaining grated Parmesan served separately.

COOK'S TIP
Italians always cook with unsalted (sweet) butter.

Risotto with Four Cheeses

This is a very rich dish. Serve it with a light, dry sparkling white wine.

Serves 8

40g/1½oz/3 tbsp butter
1 small onion, finely chopped
1.2 litres/2 pints/5 cups vegetable stock
350g/12oz/1¾ cups risotto rice
200ml/7fl oz/scant 1 cup dry white wine
50g/2oz/½ cup grated Gruyère cheese
50g/2oz/½ cup diced taleggio cheese
50g/2oz/½ cup diced Gorgonzola cheese
50g/2oz/⅔ cup freshly grated Parmesan cheese
salt and ground black pepper
chopped fresh flat leaf parsley, to garnish

1 Melt the butter in a large, heavy pan or deep frying pan. Add the onion and cook over a low heat, stirring occasionally, for about 4–5 minutes, until softened and lightly browned. Meanwhile, pour the stock into a separate pan, bring to the boil, then lower the heat to a simmer.

2 Add the rice to the pan with the onion, stir until the grains are coated with butter and starting to swell and burst, then add the wine. Stir until it stops sizzling and most of it has been absorbed by the rice.

3 Pour in a little of the hot stock. Season with salt and ground black pepper to taste. Stir the rice over a low heat until all the stock has been absorbed.

4 Gradually add the remaining stock, a little at a time, allowing the rice to absorb the liquid before adding more, and stirring constantly. After about 20–25 minutes, the rice will be tender and the risotto will be creamy.

5 Turn off the heat under the pan, then add the Gruyère, taleggio, Gorgonzola and 30ml/2 tbsp of the Parmesan. Stir gently until the cheeses have melted, then taste and adjust the seasoning, if necessary. Spoon the risotto into a warm serving bowl and garnish with parsley. Serve the remaining Parmesan separately.

Roasted Tomato and Mozzarella Salad

Roasting the tomatoes brings out their sweetness and adds a new dimension to this salad. Make the basil oil just before serving to retain its fresh flavour and lovely vivid colour.

Serves 4

olive oil, for brushing
6 large plum tomatoes
2 fresh mozzarella cheese balls, cut into 8–12 slices
salt and ground black pepper
fresh basil leaves, to garnish

For the basil oil
25 fresh basil leaves
60ml/4 tbsp extra virgin olive oil
1 garlic clove, crushed

1 Preheat the oven to 200°C/400°F/Gas 6 and brush a baking sheet with olive oil. Cut the tomatoes in half lengthways and remove and discard the seeds. Place the tomato halves, skin side down, on the baking sheet, brush with a little oil and roast for about 20 minutes, or until the tomatoes are very tender but still retain their shape.

2 Meanwhile, make the basil oil. Place the basil leaves, olive oil and garlic in a food processor or blender and process until smooth. You will need to scrape down the sides once or twice to make sure that the mixture is processed properly. Transfer to a bowl, cover with clear film (plastic wrap) and chill until required.

3 For each serving, place the tomato halves on top of two or three slices of mozzarella and drizzle over the basil oil. Season to taste with salt and pepper. Garnish with fresh basil leaves and serve immediately.

Mixed Herb Salad with Toasted Mixed Seeds

This simple salad is the perfect antidote to a rich, heavy meal, as it contains fresh herbs that can ease the digestion. Balsamic vinegar adds a rich, sweet taste to the dressing, but red or white wine vinegar could be used instead.

Serves 4

90g/3½oz/4 cups mixed salad leaves
50g/2oz/2 cups mixed salad herbs, such as coriander (cilantro), parsley, basil, chervil and rocket (arugula)
45ml/3 tbsp pumpkin seeds
45ml/3 tbsp sunflower seeds

For the dressing
60ml/4 tbsp extra virgin olive oil
15ml/1 tbsp balsamic vinegar
2.5ml/½ tsp Dijon mustard
salt and ground black pepper

1 To make the dressing, combine the ingredients in a bowl or screw-top jar. Mix with a small whisk or fork, or shake well, until completely combined.

2 Put the salad leaves and herb leaves in a large bowl. Toss with your fingers to mix together.

3 Toast the pumpkin and sunflower seeds in a dry frying pan over a medium heat for about 2 minutes, until golden, tossing frequently to prevent them from burning. Leave the seeds to cool slightly before sprinkling them over the salad.

4 Pour the dressing over the salad and toss with your hands until the leaves are well coated, then serve.

Index

asparagus: asparagus and egg terrine, 39
  asparagus and orange salad, 84
  grilled vegetable terrine, 36
  marinated asparagus and langoustines, 63
aubergines: aubergine and smoked mozzarella rolls, 88
  Greek aubergine and spinach pie, 54
  vegetable tarte tatin, 52
avocados: avocado and smoked fish salad, 74
  prawn, egg and avocado mousses, 32
  tricolor salad, 85

basil: clam and basil soup, 24
beans: cannellini bean and rosemary bruschetta, 59
branade of salt cod, 35
breaded sole batons, 70
broccoli soup with garlic toast, 13

Caesar salad, 73
cannellini bean and rosemary bruschetta, 59
capers: marinated feta cheese with capers, 58
chanterelles: tortellini chanterelle broth, 15
cheese: aubergine and smoked mozzarella rolls, 88
  crab and ricotta tartlets, 47
  creamy courgette and Dolcelatte soup, 19
  fried rice balls stuffed with mozzarella, 89
  goat's cheese salad, 83
  Greek aubergine and spinach pie, 54
  leek and onion tartlets, 51
  marinated feta cheese with capers, 58
  panzanella salad, 86
  pears and Stilton, 82
  risotto with four cheeses, 93
  roasted tomato and mozzarella salad, 94
  tricolor salad, 85
  twice-baked Gruyère and potato soufflés, 43
  wild mushroom and fontina tarts, 49
cherries: Hungarian sour cherry soup, 18
chicken: chicken bitki, 79
  chicken liver pâté with garlic, 30
  yakitori chicken, 78
chilled prawn and cucumber soup, 22
chilled tomato and sweet pepper soup, 11
chillies: courgette fritters with chilli jam, 87
clams: clam and basil soup, 24
  mussels and clams with lemon grass, 64
cod: branade of salt cod, 35
cold cucumber and yogurt soup, 10
courgettes (zucchinis): courgette fritters with chilli jam, 87
  creamy courgette and Dolcelatte soup, 19
  grilled vegetable terrine, 36
  tomato and courgette timbales, 90
crab: crab and ricotta tartlets, 47
  hot crab soufflés, 42
creamy courgette and Dolcelatte soup, 19

cucumber: chilled prawn and cucumber soup, 22
  cold cucumber and yogurt soup, 10
  salade Niçoise, 72

deep-fried whitebait, 69

eggs: asparagus and egg terrine, 39
  egg and salmon puff parcels, 56
  poached eggs Florentine, 91
  prawn, egg and avocado mousses, 32
  tomato and courgette timbales, 90
fish soup with rouille, 25
French onion and morel soup, 16
fresh tomato soup, 293
fried rice balls stuffed with mozzarella, 89
fried squid, 66

garlic: broccoli soup with garlic toast, 16
  chicken liver pâté with garlic, 30
  garlic prawns in filo tarts, 46
  Spanish garlic soup, 14
  stuffed garlic mushrooms with prosciutto, 75
goat's cheese salad, 83
Greek aubergine and spinach pie, 54
griddled tomatoes on soda bread, 50
grilled scallops with brown butter, 66
grilled vegetable terrine, 36

haddock: haddock and smoked salmon terrine, 40
  smoked haddock pâté, 29
herbed liver pâté pie, 31
hot crab soufflés, 42
hot-and-sour soup, 21
Hungarian sour cherry soup, 18

langoustines: marinated asparagus and langoustines, 63
leek and onion tartlets, 51
lemon grass: mussels and clams with lemon grass, 64
lemon sole: breaded sole batons, 70

mackerel: avocado and smoked fish salad, 74
Malaysian prawn laksa, 23
marinated asparagus and langoustines, 63
marinated feta cheese with capers, 58
melon and prosciutto salad, 76
mixed herb salad with toasted mixed seeds, 94
monkfish: three-colour fish kebabs, 71
morels: French onion and morel soup, 16
mousses: prawn, egg and avocado mousses, 32
  sea trout mousse, 33
mushrooms: French onion and morel soup, 13
  mushroom salad with prosciutto, 77
  stuffed garlic mushrooms with prosciutto, 75
  wild mushroom and fontina tarts, 49
mussels and clams with lemon grass, 64

onions: French onion and morel soup, 16
  leek and onion tartlets, 51
oranges: asparagus and orange salad, 84

panzanella salad, 86
pasta: tortellini chanterelle broth, 15

pâté: chicken liver pâté with garlic, 30
  herbed liver pâté pie, 31
  smoked haddock pâté, 29
  smoked salmon pâté, 28
pears: pear and watercress soup, 12
  pears and Stilton, 82
pesto: scallop-stuffed roast peppers with pesto, 65
poached eggs Florentine, 91
pork: herbed liver pâté pie, 31
potatoes: twice-baked Gruyère and potato soufflés, 43
potted salmon with lemon and dill, 34
prawns (shrimp): chilled prawn and cucumber soup, 22
  garlic prawns in filo tarts, 46
  Malaysian prawn laksa, 23
  prawn cocktail, 42
  prawn, egg and avocado mousses, 32
  Thai-style seafood turnovers, 57
  tiger prawns with mint, dill and lime, 48
prosciutto: melon and prosciutto salad, 76
  mushroom salad with prosciutto, 77
  stuffed garlic mushrooms with prosciutto, 75

red (bell) peppers: chilled tomato and sweet pepper soup, 11
  grilled vegetable terrine, 36
  roast pepper terrine, 38
  scallop-stuffed roast peppers with pesto, 65
  vegetable tarte tatin, 52
rice: fried rice balls stuffed with mozzarella, 89
  risotto alla Milanese, 92
  risotto with four cheeses, 93
  smoked salmon and rice salad parcels, 69
risotto: risotto alla Milanese, 92
  risotto with four cheeses, 93
roast pepper terrine, 38
roasted tomato and mozzarella salad, 94
rosemary: cannellini bean and rosemary bruschetta, 59

salade Niçoise, 72
salads: asparagus and orange salad, 84
  avocado and smoked fish salad, 74
  Caesar salad, 73
  goat's cheese salad, 83
  melon and prosciutto salad, 76
  mixed herb salad with toasted mixed seeds, 94
  mushroom salad with prosciutto, 77
  panzanella salad, 86
  roasted tomato and mozzarella salad, 94
  salade Niçoise, 72
  tricolor salad, 85
salmon: egg and salmon puff parcels, 56
  haddock and smoked salmon terrine, 40
  smoked salmon and rice salad parcels, 68
  smoked salmon pâté, 28
  three-colour fish kebabs, 71
scallops: grilled scallops with brown butter, 66
  scallop-stuffed roast peppers with pesto, 65
sea trout mousse, 33

smoked haddock pâté, 29
smoked salmon and rice salad parcels, 68
smoked salmon pâté, 28
soufflés: hot crab soufflés, 42
  twice-baked Gruyère and potato soufflés, 43
sour cream: Hungarian sour cherry soup, 18
Spanish garlic soup, 14
spinach: Greek aubergine and spinach pie, 54
  poached eggs Florentine, 91
  spinach and tofu soup, 20
squid: fried squid, 66
stuffed garlic mushrooms with prosciutto, 75
swordfish: three-colour fish kebabs, 71

tartlets: crab and ricotta tartlets, 47
  garlic prawns in filo tarts, 46
  leek and onion tartlets, 51
tarts: wild mushroom and fontina tarts, 49
terrines: asparagus and egg terrine, 39
  grilled vegetable terrine, 36
  haddock and smoked salmon terrine, 40
  roast pepper terrine, 38
Thai-style seafood turnovers, 57
three-colour fish kebabs, 71
tiger prawns with mint, dill and lime, 48
tofu: spinach and tofu soup, 20
tomatoes: chilled tomato and sweet pepper soup, 11
  fresh tomato soup, 17
  griddled tomatoes on soda bread, 50
  panzanella salad, 86
  roasted tomato and mozzarella salad, 94
  tomato and courgette timbales, 90
  tricolor salad, 85
  vegetable tarte tatin, 52
tricolor salad, 85
tuna: salade Niçoise, 72
twice-baked Gruyère and potato soufflés, 43

vegetable tarte tatin, 52

watercress: pear and watercress soup, 12
whitebait: deep-fried whitebait, 69
wild mushroom and fontina tarts, 49

yakitori chicken, 78
yogurt: cold cucumber and yogurt soup, 10